CREATIVE CROCHET

CREATIVE CROCHET

BY NICKI HITZ EDSON AND ARLENE STIMMEL

WATSON-GUPTILL PUBLICATIONS, NEW YORK

PITMAN PUBLISHING, LONDON

First published 1973 in the United States and Canada by Watson-Guptill Publications,
a division of Billboard Publications, Inc.,
One Astor Plaza, New York, N.Y. 10036

Published simultaneously in Great Britain by Sir Isaac Pitman & Sons Ltd.,
39 Parker Street, Kingsway, London WC2B 5PB
U.K. ISBN 0-273-00413-1

Manufactured in U.S.A.

Library of Congress Cataloging in Publication Data
Edson, Nicki Hitz, 1941–
    Creative crochet.

    Bibliography: p.
    1. Crocheting. I. Stimmel, Arlene, 1945–
joint author. II. Title.
TT820.E46 1973   746.4'3   73-6784
ISBN 0-8230-1040-6

First Printing, 1973

Acknowledgments

We'd like to thank Julie Schafler for showing our work and modeling for most the photographs; Sharron Hedges for the beautiful line drawings; Janet Lipkin Decker for moral support and inspiration; Diane Casella Hines for her enthusiasm, and Jennifer Place for her solace when our slides were stolen two days before the book was due at the publishers. Also, there wouldn't be a book without all the people who generously contributed their work, and we'd especially like to thank them.

Photographs by Nicki Hitz Edson

Clothing diagrams by Arlene Stimmel

Fancy Stitches diagrams by Nicki Edson

All other diagrams by Sharron Hedges

For British readers: the names of the basic crochet stitches used in this book differ slightly from those used in standard British patterns. The key below provides the necessary equivalents.

Stitch given here	British equivalent
Single crochet	Double crochet
Double crochet	Treble crochet
Half-double crochet	Half-treble crochet
Treble crochet	Double treble crochet

Contents

Introduction, 8

1. Materials, 10

Hooks, 11
Choosing Your Yarn, 12
Combining Different Fibers, 12
Wool Yarn, 12
Miscellaneous Equipment, 13
Yarn Chart, 15

2. Groundwork, 18

Slip Knot, 19
Chain Stitch, 19

3. Basic Stitches, 26

Single Crochet, 26
Double Crochet, 26
Half-Double Crochet, 27
Treble Crochet, 27
Joining Yarn, 27
Slip Stitch, 27

4. Fancy Stitches, 44

Shell Stitch Sampler, 45
Filet Pattern Sampler, 45
Picot and Bar Stitch Sampler, 47
Accent Stitch Sampler, 47
Joining Two Pieces of Crochet, 47
Border Stitches, 47

5. Shapes, 64

Basic Shapes, 65
Unusual Shapes, 66
Pillow Sampler, 66

6. Clothing, 82

Crocheting without a Pattern, 84
Considerations Before You Start, 84
Blocking, 86

7. Color, Design, and Ideas, 98

Color Plates, 105

8. Sculpture, 118

9. Junk and Mixed Media, 128

Beads, 129
Crochet and Other Materials, 129

Suppliers List, 138

Bibliography, 141

Index, 142

Introduction

Everyone has known someone who's crocheted—grandma, aunt, or mom—but they always seemed to make the same things over and over. Doilies, afghans, and baby booties. Their work was beautiful, but all the doilies looked pretty much the same and the afghans always had black borders. Perhaps you've asked yourself why crochet has to be so limited? The answer is, it doesn't. There's no end to what you can crochet. In fact, we can't think of anything that *can't* be crocheted. Here are just a few of the things that have passed through friends' hooks in recent years, most three-dimensional: all kinds of wearing apparel—vests, hats, dresses, a pair of chaps, shirts, fantasy costumes; animals real and imagined—frogs, turtles, horses, swans, dragons, and an 18-foot turkey; planets, stars, clouds, flowers, mushrooms, a forest, houses, masks, giant dolls and tiny dolls, puppets; and even a steak dinner, complete with potatoes, salad, and a cup of coffee.

More and more people are discovering this old craft as a medium in which to express themselves. It's easy, relatively fast, and best of all, in these nomadic times, it's portable. You can carry it with you anywhere. There's no need to determine exactly how a piece is going to look before you begin; it grows as you go along, adding to itself. You can crochet in any direction, up, down or sideways, and one stitch, design, stripe, or shape leads to another. If you like having more control, however, you can plan your design first with a drawing. You'll be amazed how versatile crochet is—you can make just about any shape.

Everyone does things for different reasons, so maybe you'd be interested to know how we started crocheting:

Arlene: I used to paint with automobile spray paints, which took about 20 minutes to dry between coats. I taught myself to crochet just so I'd have something to do during these time lags. Soon I was crocheting more and painting less. At first I made only simple things, but before I knew it, yarn had replaced paint as my medium and I wanted to make paintings people could wear. I was hooked.

Nicki: My mother taught me to do simple stuff, single crochet hats and vests, on a summer visit about six years ago. But when I saw a crocheted hanging by Walter Nottingham in the Museum of Modern Art, I couldn't believe it! I knew then that anything could be crocheted.

And so I began to make houses that were small stuffed childrens' toys. One got too big and round so I cut it in half and made my first outrageous hat. Hats turned into helmets, helmets into masks, and it spiraled on and on.

We hope you picked up this book because you too want to take crocheting beyond doilies, afghans and step-by-step patterns. In fact, a friend wanted to call the book, "Beyond the Oily Doily."

We'll start out by looking at the materials available and the basic techniques and stitches. Then we'll go into shapes and how to put them together, color, design and ideas, making clothes, and three-dimensional crochet. And if you're already involved in other crafts (or want to be) you can combine crochet with macramé, leathercraft, ceramics, metalwork, weaving, knitting, needlepoint, appliqué, etc.

As a method for learning the stitches, we've invented samplers for you to work, and we hope that you'll use them to create beautiful things of your own. We suggest that you do the samplers in order, because they all draw something from the ones before. By the time you finish the last one, you'll know quite a bit about crochet, certainly enough to get you going. And from there, who knows what can happen?

Keep in mind three things as you study this book:

1. Crocheting is a logical process; everything you do makes sense.

2. Make mistakes; they help you learn and you can easily rip them out.

3. Don't be afraid; with patience and practice you can do it.

1. Materials

Crochet Hooks *in a range of sizes with two yarn needles in the center.*

All you need to crochet are two very portable things: a hook and some yarn.

Hooks

Crochet hooks come in different sizes to be used with different yarns. There are very small hooks made of steel that are used with very thin thread to make delicate laces, doilies, and intricate tablecloths. These hooks are numbered, and they range in size from 14, the smallest, to 00 (zero zero), the largest. Just looking at these hooks makes your eyes hurt—the only one you'll probably ever use is a 00. Then there are larger hooks made of aluminum or plastic that are used for most of the work done today in wool and other heavier materials. They are lettered, ranging in size from C, the smallest, to K, the largest. (For some strange reason there's no size A or B, and size D is almost impossible to find, although it does exist.) For very bulky yarn there are giant hooks about ½″ thick, lettered P, Q, R, and S.

Aluminum hooks are preferable to plastic ones because they're stronger and the hook end is round and smooth. The plastic ones are cheaply made and often have burrs which can catch on the yarn. Good hooks cost about 50¢, so there's no reason to skimp on quality.

The size hook you use depends on several things. The first thing to consider is the weight of the yarn. For example, for average-size yarn, say a thin rug yarn, we would use an F or G hook. Generally, small hooks are used for thin yarn and larger ones for thicker, heavier yarns. But there are no hard and fast rules—Mark Dittrick makes beautiful tight fabric by using a heavy yarn with a very small hook. (See his work in the photo opposite.)

The second consideration is how loose or tight you want your stitches to be. For example, if your stitches are too loose, you can switch to a smaller hook and the work will tighten up. If your stitches are too tight, you can switch to a larger hook and the work will be looser. Use whatever size you need to get the effect you want. If you're not sure, it's always a good idea to work up swatches using several hooks of

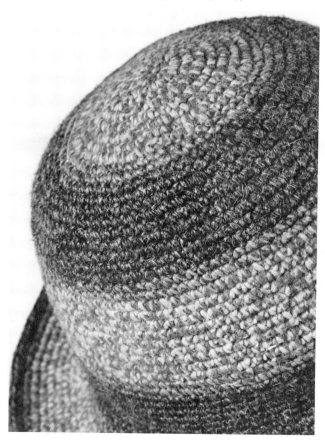

Detail of a Wool Hat by Mark Dittrick. Mark used a size 0 (zero) steel hook, 2-ply weaving wool, and single crochet to get the tight effect.

different sizes and see which you like best.

Because you can't always determine your needs beforehand (and you'll probably want that F hook on Sunday night when the stores are closed), it's a good idea to shell out the $4.50 and have a complete supply of aluminum hooks on hand. Then one of your first projects can be crocheting something to put them in.

Choosing Your Yarn

For practice pieces and experiments you can use any old yarn, but once you've decided to make something specific, that's where the fun begins. There are so many incredible yarns to choose from that deciding which one to use can be the hardest part of a project. There are two ways to approach this—let the project inspire the yarn, or let the yarn inspire the project. For instance, you might decide to make a delicate tank top that you'll wear without anything under it. Right away you eliminate the scratchy, heavy materials, but you're still not sure exactly what you want to use. So you search through the yarn shops and your catalogs until you find just the right soft yarn in just the right color(s) and then

A Man's Necktie done with four strands of very thin yarn worked together and changed in mid-row for a tweedy effect. This is another of Mark Dittrick's super-tight pieces in single crochet.

you get to work. The project has inspired the yarn.

On the other hand, you may have collected quite a stockpile of yarn from browsing through a shop and finding an unexpected bargain. Or you might see a catalog with glorious things in it and they're so inexpensive that you order a couple of pounds. As your collection grows and you keep looking over what you have (like any collector), you decide that the soft wool you got from Iceland would make a fantastic scarf for your mountain-climbing friend, and then you get to work. The yarn has inspired the project.

Combining Different Fibers

Another thing to consider is combining several different materials in the same project. If you're making a rayon vest you might want to add some cotton to cut the sheen and provide a change in texture. Different types of wool can be used successfully in the same project to give an added richness. Whatever yarns you use, always be conscious of quality—it just doesn't make sense to spend a lot of time making something with cheap worsted from the dime store.

Wool Yarn

Because wool is by far the most popular and versatile fiber, we'd like to give you some background information on its qualities and how it's made.

Wool comes in many thicknesses, twists, and textures; it dyes well and comes in soft, subtle colors as well as bright, vibrant ones. It can be soft enough for a baby's sweater or coarse enough for a fishermans' sweater made to last for several generations. It has a natural elasticity, and when knitted or crocheted the air spaces formed make it one of the warmest fabrics known.

Wool comes from sheep raised especially for their fleece. In different parts of the world, different breeds are raised, and the local wool reflects the environment. What the sheep eat, the type of weather, the roughness of the terrain, and the time the sheep are shorn all make a difference in the final product. It's so incredible that the yarn you work with actually comes from grass—the sheep eat, grow wool, and keep providing it as long as they live. And they don't have to lose their lives to provide it— only a little dignity as they run around pink and naked after shearing.

Although you may never get involved in the process of converting raw fleece to yarn, it's interesting to know something about it. The sheep are shorn in full fleece (one big piece) several times a year. The fleece are then pulled apart and the fibers sorted. As in a single fleece, the fibers are of different qualities and lengths and the texture and quality of the fibers varies from one breed to another.

After sorting, the raw fibers are cleaned to remove twigs, thistles, and other vegetable matter. Then they're scoured (sheep talk for washed) in preparation for dyeing, which, when done at this stage of the game, is called dyeing "in the fleece." Certain types of yarn, such as "fisherman yarn" is not scoured because the lanolin from the fleece gives the yarn its unique waterproof quality. Yarn with the lanolin still in can't be dyed because the oil won't let the dye penetrate the fibers. That's why authentic fishermans' sweaters are always a natural color (off-white, gray, light brown, dark brown, or black).

Now the fibers are ready to be spun into yarn. First they must be untangled and this step depends on their length. When prepared by hand, the longer fibers are "combed" with what resembles a 2 x 4 board with 3″ nails sticking vertically out of one end. Shorter fibers are "carded" with what resembles two steel-toothed dog combs stroked in opposite directions with the fibers passing from one to the other until all the tangles are out and the fibers look like gossamer.

After the fibers are either combed or carded, they are made into rolls with a light pressure from the heel of the hand (similar to making snakes with clay) and are ready for the actual spinning. Basically, spinning is twisting the fibers as they come from the roll, forming what we call yarn. This can be done with either a hand spindle or a spinning wheel. The yarn can be used at this stage, or several strands can be twisted together to form a "plyed" yarn. When you see a "4-ply" yarn it means that four strands have been twisted together to form a thicker yarn.

When you buy yarn that has a dye lot on the label, it means that the yarn has been dyed after it's been spun. The color varies from dye lot to dye lot so it's a good idea to buy as much as you think you'll need from the same lot. Or why not buy some undyed natural yarn and try dyeing it yourself? If you choose chemical dyes, follow the directions on the package. If you want to go all out with vegetable dyes, Alma Lesch's book *Vegetable Dyeing* is very good.

It would be impossible to explain every type of yarn available to you, so the chart at the end of this chapter is an attempt to familiarize you with the major fibers, descriptions of the yarns made from them, and how they can be used.

Miscellaneous Equipment

Aside from hooks and yarn there are several other things you'll find helpful to have. Get several sizes of blunt-ended steel yarn

needles for weaving loose ends into the finished piece of work. You'll also need a pair of small, sharp scissors. And there are two pieces of equipment that you may not think you need, but they make life with yarn a lot easier—a yarn winder and a swift.

A yarn winder is a clever gadget that makes up to 4-ounce balls of yarn in about a quarter of the time it takes by hand. A crank turns a geared spindle and the yarn collects on the spindle. If you're making balls from a spool or cone of yarn, you just set it on the floor, clamp the winder to a table, and crank away.

If you want to wind a ball from a skein, then you need a swift. This is a wooden tool made up of a central shaft with four accordion-like arms that adjust to the size of the skein. When stretched out, they hold the skein securely in place and as you crank the winder, the swift turns, feeding the yarn to the winder. It all goes very fast and it's much less frustrating than winding balls by hand. Check the Suppliers List on page 138 for places to get these.

A Yarn Winder and Swift are two very helpful tools for winding yarn into balls. Note the position of the hands while winding.

YARN CHART

Name	Description	Advantages or Disadvantages	Uses	Sources
WOOL				
WORSTED	Soft, smooth, medium thick, very stretchy.	Soft touching skin, good range of colors.	Skirts, tops, dresses, vests, hats, scarves, boots, pillows, afghans, bedspreads.	Yarn stores.
RUG YARN (weaving yarn)	Coarse, rough, scratchy, medium thick, no stretch.	Very strong, rough on skin	Afghans, bedspreads, rugs, wall hangings, vests, coats, boots, pillows, lampshades, flowerpot hangers, curtains, bags, belts, sculpture.	Rug factories, weaving supply houses.
RYA RUG YARN	Coarse, plyed and twisted, medium thick, some stretch.	Strong, rough on skin, many colors.	Vests, coats, boots, pillows, lampshades, flowerpot holders, curtains, bedspreads, rugs, wall hangings, sculpture, bags, belts.	Import stores, Scandinavia.*
MATT YARN	Coarse, one ply, medium thick, some stretch.	Strong, rough on skin.	Skirts, vests, coats, boots, pillows, lampshades, flowerpot holders, curtains, bedspreads, rugs, wall hangings, sculpture, belts, bags.	Import stores, Scandinavia.*
COWHAIR	Coarse, rough, scratchy, one ply, medium thick, some stretch.	Strong, rough on skin.	Skirts, vests, coats, boots, pillows, lampshades, flowerpot holders, curtains, bedspreads, rugs, wall hangings, sculpture, belts, bags.	Import stores, Scandinavia.*
SCOTTISH YARN	Soft, thin, has stretch.	Subtle, heathery colors	Skirts, tops, dresses, hats, scarves.	Import stores, Scotland.*
IRISH	Medium coarse, varies in thickness, natural colors.	Warm, oily.	Skirts, vests, shawls, coats, hats, scarves, mittens, boots, pillows, afghans, bedspreads, rugs, wall hangings, sculpture.	Import stores, Ireland.*
FISHERMAN'S YARN	Medium coarse, medium thick to heavy, natural colors.	Natural oils left in yarn.	Skirts, vests, shawls, coats, hats, scarves, mittens, boots, pillows, afghans, bedspreads, rugs, wall hangings, sculpture.	Import stores, Ireland.*

*can be ordered by mail.

Name	Description	Advantages or Disadvantages	Uses	Sources
ALPACA and MOHAIR	Very soft, fuzzy, thin to medium.	Mohair, from goats. Difficult to pull out once crocheted.	Skirts, tops, dresses, vests, shawls, coats, hats, scarves, boots, pillows, afghans, bedspreads, wall hangings, sculpture.	Import stores, South America.* yarn stores.
CASHMERE	Fine, very soft, stretchy.	Warm, not strong.	Skirts, dresses, tops, vests, shawls, hats, scarves, pillows.	Import stores.

COTTON

Name	Description	Advantages or Disadvantages	Uses	Sources
SPEED CROSHEEN DOUBLE QUICK	Thin, braided, no stretch.	Works smoothly, comes in colors.	Skirts, tops, dresses, vests, pillows, lampshades, flowerpot holders, curtains, bags, swim suits, belts.	Yarn stores.
COTTON THREAD	Thin, plyed and twisted, no stretch.	Good colors.	Skirts, tops, dresses, vests, pillows, lampshades, flowerpot holders, curtains, bags, swim suits, belts.	Yarn stores.
COTTON STRING	Thickness varies, strong, no stretch.	Very strong, few colors.	Vests, pillows, lampshades, flowerpot holders, wall hangings, sculpture, bags, belts.	Hardware stores, yarn stores.

LINEN

Name	Description	Advantages or Disadvantages	Uses	Sources
FINE LINEN	Soft, strong, no stretch.	Good colors and natural.	Skirts, tops, dresses, vests, shawls, pillows, lampshades, flowerpot holders, curtains, wall hangings, sculpture.	Weaving supply houses.
COARSE LINEN	Thick, heavy, twist varies, strong, no stretch.	Natural colors only, very strong.	Pillows, lampshades, flowerpot holders, wall hangings, sculpture, bags, belts.	Marine supply stores.

Name	Description	Advantages or Disadvantages	Uses	Sources
SYNTHETICS				
CORDÉ	Rayon, wrapped around cotton, shiny.	Unravels, does not wear well, good to mix with other yarns.	Vests, pillows, lampshades, curtains, wall hangings, sculpture, bags, belts.	Specialty yarn stores.
SOUTACHE	Rayon wrapped around two strands of cotton which makes it flat.	Wears better than corde.	Vests, pillows, lampshades, curtains, wall hangings, sculpture, bags, belts.	Specialty yarn stores.
CHAINETTE	Rayon chained, very pliable, slippery, shiny.	Slipperiness is hard to work with, finished product very stretchy.	Tops, vests, shawls, lampshades, curtains.	Specialty yarn stores.
RAYON RIBBON	Rayon braided into flat ribbon, shiny, slippery.	Soft when washed, good to mix with other yarns.	Tops, vests, dresses, shawls, hats, pillows, lampshades, curtains, wall hangings, sculpture, belts.	Specialty yarn stores.
PARADISE	Acetate chained, bouncy, stretchy.	Good colors, washable.	Skirts, tops, dresses, vests, shawls, hats, pillows, bedspreads, rugs, toys, bags, belts.	Yarn stores.
CHENILLE	Velvet-like	Soft texture.	Skirts, tops, dresses, vests, hats, pillows, wall hangings, sculpture.	Yarn stores.
METALLICS	Plastic, wrapped around cotton.	Too stiff for clothing, good for highlights.	Mix with other materials.	Yarn stores.
MIXTURES				
BOUCLÉ	Bumpy, soft, wool, mohair and synthetics.	Difficult to see stitches, good texture.	Hats, scarves, boots.	Yarn stores.
RUG YARN	Thick, stretch, cotton-rayon mix.	Good for beginners.	Vests, coats, hats, pillows, bedspreads, rugs, toys, bags, belts.	Yarn stores.

2. Groundwork

Woolen Holders *for small items by Mark Dittrick. These were made with simple single and double crochet stitches worked in stripes. Each has a loop on the back so they can slip onto a belt.*

We've been crocheting for quite awhile and some of our pieces look pretty wierd. When people look at it their first reaction is usually, "It looks so complicated, how on earth did you do it?" And we inevitably say, "It's only a few stitches, it's really not that hard!" All the complex-looking designs are really the result of a few basic, simple stitches, logically organized. With this approach, you don't need patterns and you can make almost anything. That's what this book is about—all you need is the desire to learn and the willingness to experiment.

This chapter starts you off at the very beginning. The next chapter goes on to explain the basic stitches. At the end of each chapter you'll find easy-to-follow, step-by-step demonstrations for each technique discussed. So if you've never crocheted before, you can learn, and if you've had experience you can brush up and maybe learn a few new things. The most important thing to remember is to relax.

Slip Knot

The very first thing to learn in crochet is how to make the slip knot that loops over the hook. Then you need to learn how to hold the hook and the yarn. The flat part of the hook is made for your fingers to hold. At first you may want to hold on very tight, but as you start working, try to relax your fingers. If you feel yourself holding on too tight, put down your work and shake your hands out as hard as you can. This is a trick taught in art school to relax cramped fingers. Also, when you're learning to hold the yarn, remember that the tension on the yarn must be uniform.

Chain Stitch

The next thing to master is the chain stitch. Every piece of crochet is started from a base of chain stitches, so it's important to practice this. Keep making long chains until your work looks even and you feel comfortable doing them. All the stitches should be the same size, and they shouldn't be either too loose or too tight. Here you'll encounter a "yarn over" (yo). This means to bring the yarn over the hook from the back to the front.

Having accomplished your chain, you already have something you can use: a chain will hold a hanging plant, tie back your hair, hold a pendant around your neck, make a pull cord for a light, and a hundred other things.

To finish off a row of chains, cut the yarn about 3″ from the hook, yarn over, and pull the loose end all the way through. This is how you finish off any piece of crochet, but you'll see more about that later.

The last basic thing to learn is how to begin working off a foundation chain. You will see that there are three ways to do it, but don't worry about perfecting all three yet. Just practice the first method. A few things should be noted about the illustrations of the stitches that you'll be following. Every other stitch is shaded so you can tell them apart easily. Also, the illustrations look exactly like your actual stitches will look. The abbreviations following the names of the stitches are the standard ones that you'll find in most patterns. The illustrations shown are for right-handed people. If you're a lefty, just reverse hands. Or follow the directions as given—a lot of lefties crochet right-handed.

Making a Slip Knot

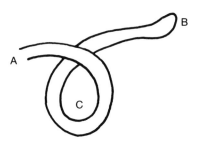

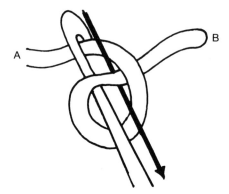

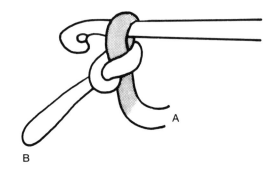

Step 1. *Lay your working yarn (A), which is the yarn from the ball, over the short end (B) of the yarn to form a loop (C).*

Step 2. *Insert your hook from the front of the loop. Pull yarn A through the loop in the direction of the arrow.*

Step 3. *Keep the loop you've just made on the hook. Pull A and B tight. You're ready to start.*

Holding the Hook and Yarn

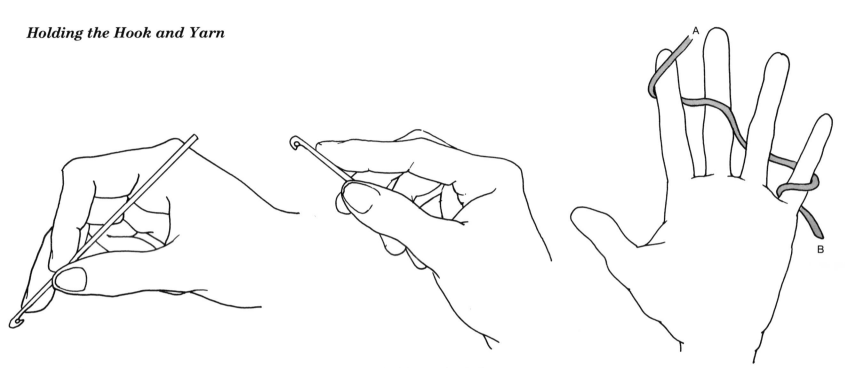

You can hold your hook the same way as you would a pencil.

You can also hold your hook between your thumb and index finger, the way an artist holds his charcoal.

You can hold the yarn by wrapping it around your pinky, over your ring finger, under your middle finger, and over your index finger. Yarn A is the working yarn; yarn B is the short end.

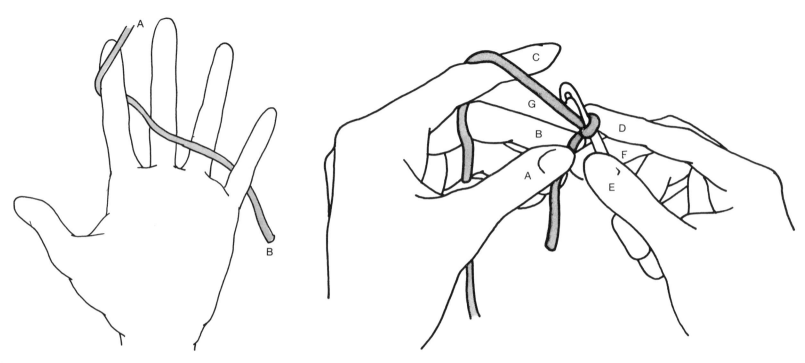

You can also hold the yarn by wrapping it over your pinky, under your ring and middle fingers, and over your index finger. Yarn A is the working yarn; yarn B is the short end.

These hands are in good working position. Fingers A and B hold the work in progress (close to the hook). Finger C controls the tension. Finger D holds the loop(s) on the hook. The yarn (G) should always make a straight line.

Making a Chain Stitch (ch)

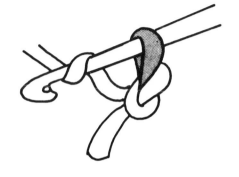

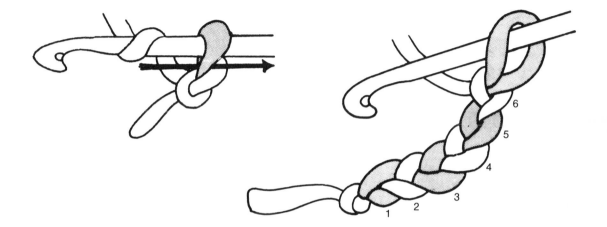

Step 1. *Yarn over.*

Step 2. *Pull the yarn through the loop on the hook in the direction of the arrow. This makes 1 chain stitch.*

By repeating Steps 1 and 2 you can make as many chain stitches as you need. Note the evenness of the 6 stitches shown here. Also notice how you count chain stitches.

Working Off a Foundation Chain

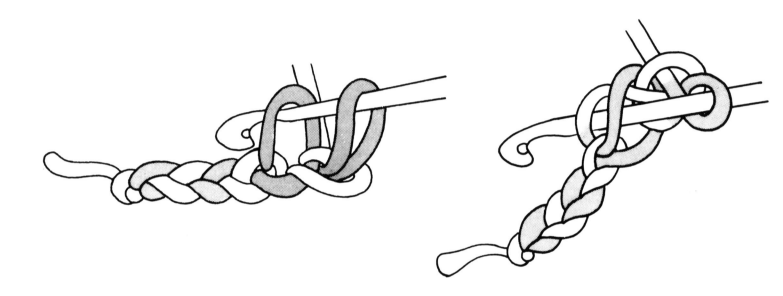

You can work off the foundation chain by picking up the top piece of each chain.

You can also work off the foundation chain by picking up the top 2 pieces of each chain.

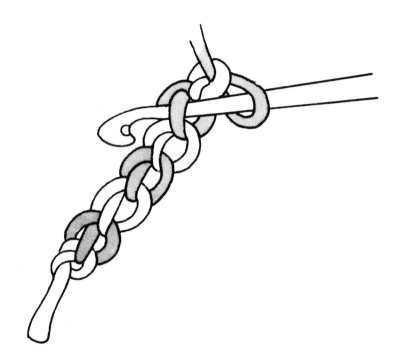

A third possibility for working off the foundation chain is to flip the chain over and pick up the back piece of each chain. This leaves a neat chain on the bottom edge of your work.

3. Basic Stitches

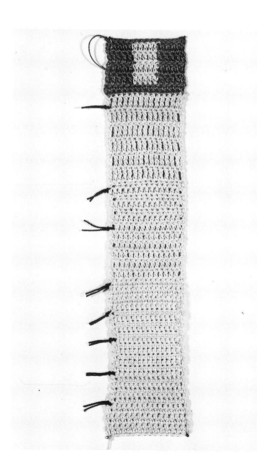

The Sampler of Basic Stitches. *This sampler was worked in cotton yarn so the differences between stitches would be easier to see.*

Instead of just making swatches of all the basic stitches, it's far more interesting to make a long sampler. This way you'll be able to practice all the stitches, see how they look together, and have samples to refer to later on. You'll also learn how to join new yarn and change colors. You should use a medium-weight yarn (knitting worsted is good) and a G or H hook. The sampler is planned to be 15 stitches wide and 56 rows long.

Single Crochet

Single crochet will be the first stitch on the sampler. It's a tight stitch and is used when you want a piece without big holes or a flat design without much surface texture. Single crochet also has several variations which can add interesting effects to a piece of work. You'll be adding the *ridge stitch*, the *Albanian stitch*, the *rib stitch*, and the *cross stitch* to the sampler. For all the vari-

ation stitches, do a regular single crochet in the first and last stitch of every row. This will keep the edges from stretching out. Also, as you work, keep counting your stitches to make sure you still have 15 stitches in each row. If you don't, don't be afraid to rip. Go back to a place where you recognize what you have and continue from there. This place will get easier to spot the more you practice.

Double Crochet

The second basic stitch in the sampler is double crochet. It's twice the height of single crochet and gives an even-textured effect. It has a bit more space between stitches than single, but not enough space to be called lacy. It's used in most of the fancy stitches you'll learn in the next chapter. Now is a good place to mention turning chains. At the end of every row of crochet, you must make a certain number of chain stitches before you turn your work and begin the next row. *The turning chains always count as the first stitch of the new row,* except in single crochet, where the one turning chain becomes part of the first stitch. This is important to remember as you're working your double crochet; otherwise you won't end up with the right number of stitches on the sampler.

Half-Double Crochet

The next basic stitch is the half-double crochet. It's easier to do once you've mastered double crochet, but in height it's between single and double. It goes faster than single crochet, gives a similar tight effect, and it's fun to do once you get the hang of it.

Treble Crochet

Treble crochet comes next. It gives you a bar that's even higher than double (think of it as three singles high). It's often used in lacy, openwork stitches. There are two variations on treble crochet that you can use if you want a very open stitch with exceptionally long bars. You're not going to add these to the sampler, but you should be aware that they exist. They are double treble and triple treble. In double treble, you yarn over 3 times, work the loops off 2 by 2, and make 5 turning chains. For triple treble, you yarn over 4 times, work the loops off 2 by 2, and make 6 turning chains.

Joining Yarn

When you've finished these basic stitches, you'll learn to end a piece of crochet, and then to join on a new piece of yarn in the beginning of the next row. There are two reasons you might want to do this: either you've run out of yarn, or you want to start using a different color. Here's a trick that will save you time at the end of a project. When you start a new ball of yarn or a new color, crochet the loose end into the row of stitches as you go along. Carry the end along for about 2″ and cut it close to the work later. This will give you fewer ends to weave in when you're done. Next you'll learn how to join a piece of yarn in the middle of a row. Your sampler will have 2 rows of single crochet in a new color joined at the beginning of the row, and then an area of double crochet with a vertical stripe in the middle (joined in mid-row).

Slip Stitch

The slip stitch is the final thing to learn. It's not really a stitch, but is often used to finish an edge neatly, or to join two pieces of crochet together. Make sure when you're finishing your sampler not to pull the slip stitches too tight or the work will buckle. Because its used to start work in the round, you'll also learn how to close a ring of chain stitches. This won't be part of your sampler, but it's important to know.

After you've finished off the ends of your sampler, your work is done. Relax with a cup of tea, a mug of beer, or a glass of wine. That wasn't so hard was it? And the more you practice the easier it will become. This first sampler will probably look awful, but before you know it your work will get neater and go faster. If you're ambitious, do this sampler over—it's good practice. Whatever you do, don't throw it out. Save it for reference later on, or for nostalgia's sake if it's the first piece of crocheting you've ever done. Savor it for awhile—you've really accomplished something—and then go on to some fancy stitches.

Single Crochet (sc)

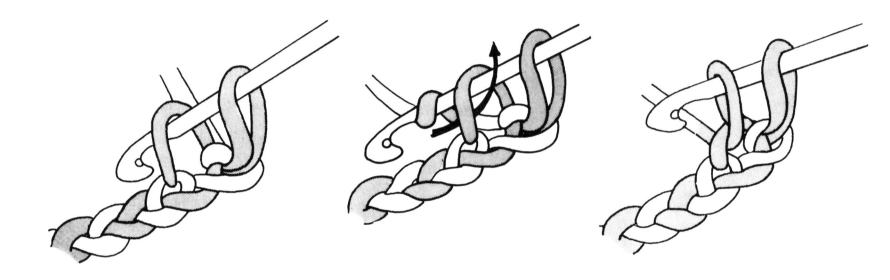

Step 1. *Chain 15 (the number of stitches on the sampler), then chain 1 extra (always with single crochet). Insert your hook from the front into the second chain from the hook. Remember, the loop on the hook never counts as a stitch.*

Step 2 A. *Yarn over. Pull the yarn through the loop of the chain in the direction of the arrow.*

Step 2 B. *Now you have 2 loops on the hook.*

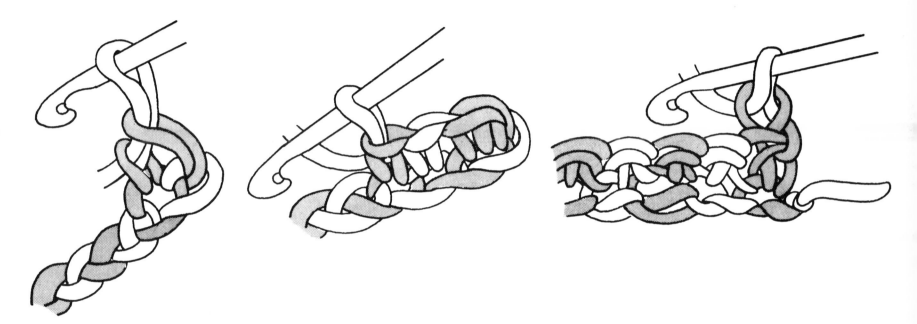

Step 3. *Yarn over. Pull the yarn through the 2 loops on the hook. 1 loop remains on the hook and you've made 1 single crochet.*

Step 4. *Do 1 single crochet in each chain.*

At the end of the row, chain 1 and turn (counter-clockwise) so the reverse side of the work is facing you. Note where you insert the hook to make the first stitch of the second row. Work the second row the same way as you did the first. Make sure you pick up both top pieces of the stitch below each time, and learn to count each stitch to make sure you still have 15 stitches. Do 6 rows of single crochet in all.

Single Crochet Variations

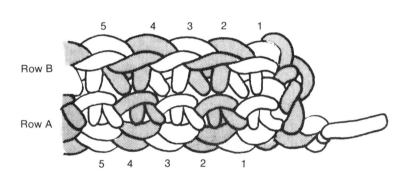

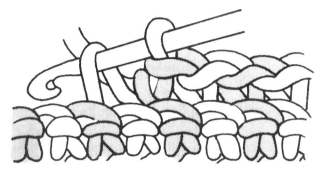

Here's an illustration of two rows of single crochet, Row A and Row B. The stitches in each row are numbered and shaded to help you count them. It's easy to count single crochet if you look down at the top of the row just completed. Notice that each stitch has a chain on top. Counting these chains gives you the number of stitches.

The Ridge Stitch is made by picking up only the **back** piece of each stitch in the previous row of single crochet. Add 6 rows of ridge stitches to your sampler.

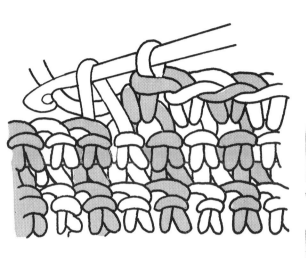

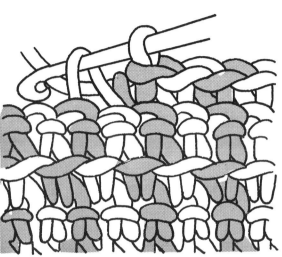

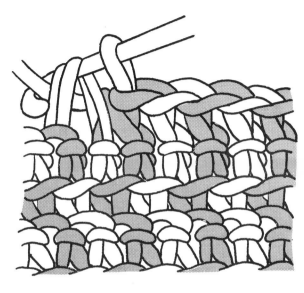

The Albanian Stitch is made by picking up only the **front** piece of each stitch in the previous row. Add 6 rows of Albanian stitches to your sampler.

The Rib Stitch is made by picking up the **back** piece of each stitch on the first row, the **front** piece of each stitch on the second row, the **back** piece on the third row, etc. It forms a raised line on the right side of the work. Add 6 rows to your sampler.

The Cross Stitch is made by picking up both pieces of each stitch (as in single crochet) but by yarning over **backwards** (from front to back). Add 6 rows to your sampler. At this point you should have 30 rows on the sampler. Count also to make sure you still have 15 stitches across.

Double Crochet (dc)

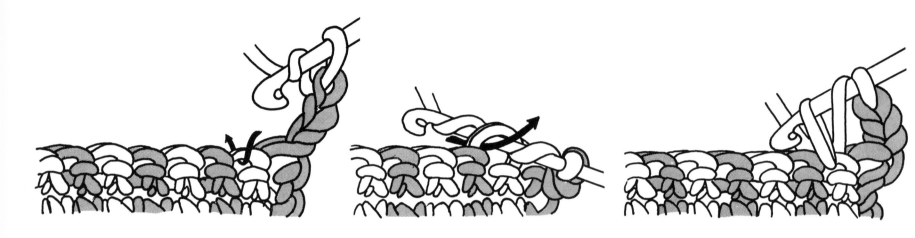

Step 1. *(A) Chain 3 at the end of the last row and turn your work. The chain 3 is the first double crochet stitch of the row you're about to do. (B) Yarn over. Insert the hook under both top pieces of the **second** stitch of the previous row in the direction of the arrow. Remember that the chain 3 is your first stitch.*

Step 2. *Yarn over. Pull the yarn through in the direction of the arrow.*

Step 3. *Now you have 3 loops on the hook.*

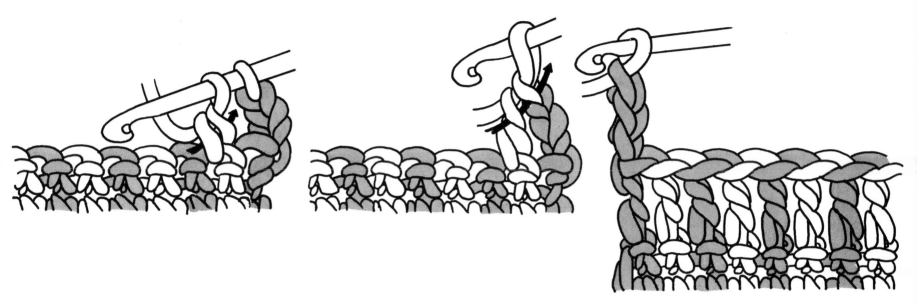

Step 4. *Yarn over. Pull the yarn through 2 loops in the direction of the arrow. You should have 2 loops left on the hook.*

Step 5. *Yarn over. Pull the yarn through the 2 remaining loops in the direction of the arrow. There is now 1 loop left on the hook and you've made 1 double crochet. Make 1 double crochet in each stitch of the previous row.*

Step 6. *At the end of the row, chain 3 and turn.*

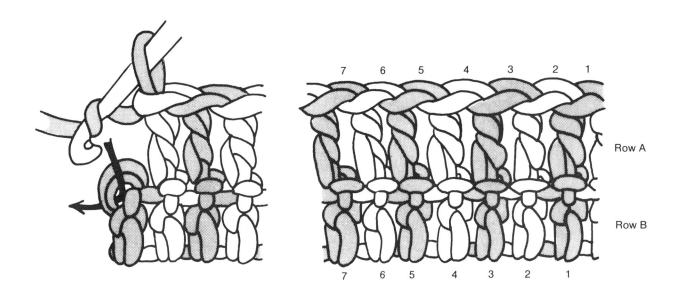

Row A

Row B

Do a second row of double crochet. The last stitch of this row must be made in the top chain of your turning chains of the first row. Add 6 rows of double crochet to your sampler.

Here's an illustration of 2 rows of double crochet, Row A and Row B. The stitches in each row are numbered and shaded to help you count them. Notice how double crochet forms a bar and is easy to count.

Half-Double Crochet (hdc)

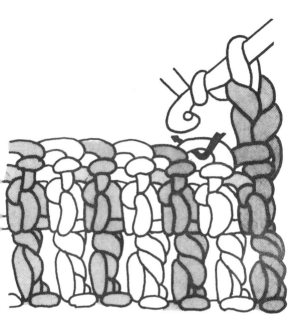 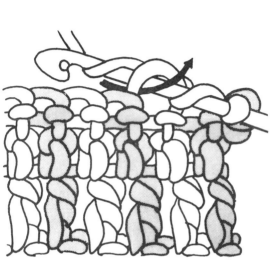 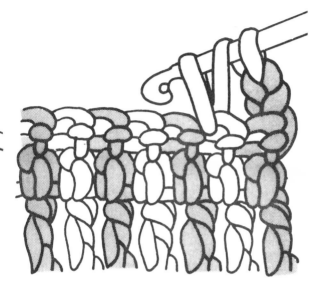

Step 1. *(A) Chain 2 at the end of the last row and turn. The chain 2 is the first half-double crochet of the row you're about to do. (B) Yarn over. Insert your hook under both top pieces of the second stitch of the previous row in the direction of the arrow. Remember that the chain 2 is your first stitch.*

Step 2. *Yarn over. Pull the yarn through in the direction of the arrow.*

Step 3. *Now you have 3 loops on the hook.*

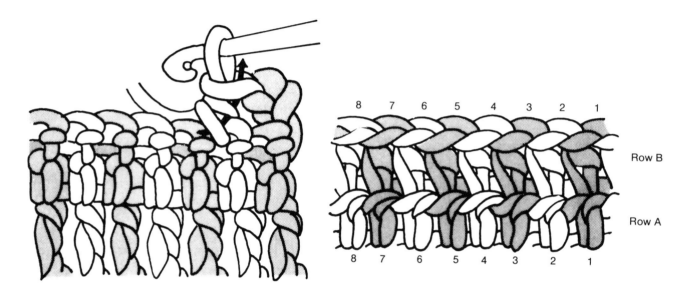

Step 4. *Yarn over. Pull the yarn through **all 3** loops at once in the direction of the arrow. If you hold your left thumb and middle finger right under the 3 loops, the yarn will slip through easily. 1 loop remains on the hook and you have made 1 half-double crochet. Add 6 rows of half-double crochet to the sampler.*

Here's an illustration of 2 rows of half-double crochet, Row A and Row B. The stitches are numbered and shaded to help you count them. Also make sure you still have 15 stitches across the row.

Treble (Triple) Crochet (tr)

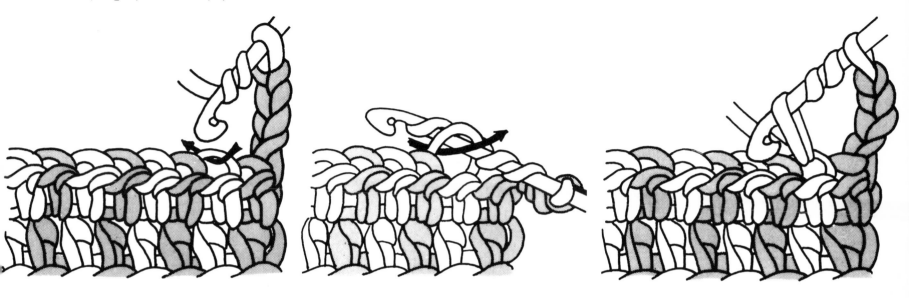

Step 1. *(A) Chain 4 at the end of the last row and turn. The chain 4 is the first treble crochet of the row you're about to do. (B) Yarn over* ***twice****. Insert the hook under both top pieces of the second stitch of the previous row in the direction of the arrow. Remember that the chain 4 is your first stitch.*

Step 2. *Yarn over. Pull the yarn through in the direction of the arrow.*

Step 3. *You now have 4 loops on the hook.*

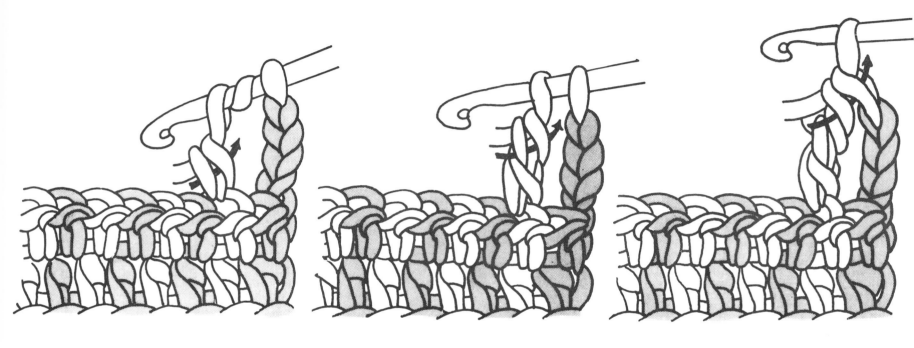

Step 4. *Yarn over. Pull the yarn through 2 loops in the direction of the arrow. You now have 3 loops on the hook.*

Step 5. *Yarn over. Pull the yarn through 2 loops in the direction of the arrow. You now have 2 loops on the hook.*

Step 6. *Yarn over. Pull the yarn through the 2 remaining loops in the direction of the arrow. You now have 1 loop on the hook and have made 1 treble crochet. Add 6 rows of stitches to your sampler. You should now have 48 rows of stitches.*

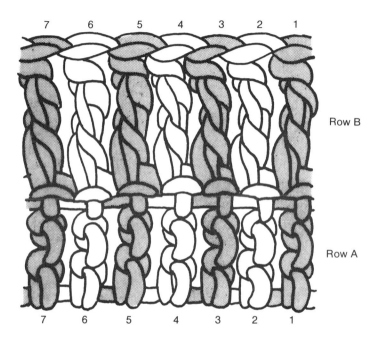

Row B

Row A

Here's an illustration of 2 rows of treble crochet, Row A and Row B. The stitches are numbered and shaded to help you count them. Note how each stitch makes a long bar and is therefore easy to count.

Step 1. Cut the yarn, leaving an end about 3″ long. Yarn over and pull the loose end through in the direction of the arrow.

Joining New Yarn

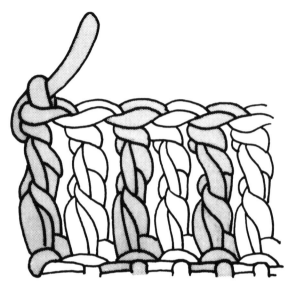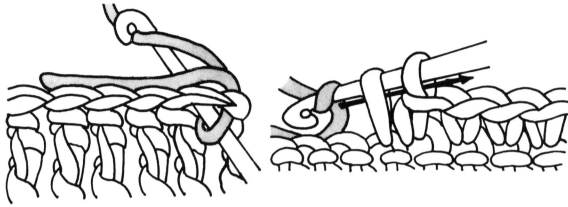

Step 2. *Pull the loose end tight—it will look like this and will keep your piece from unraveling. End your sampler off in this way.*

To join a new yarn at the beginning of a row, first insert your hook at the beginning of the row just as if you were making a stitch. Pull the loose end of the new yarn all the way through, leaving a 3" end. Tie a knot, and insert the hook again in the same place. Pull a loop through with the new yarn, and then make the right number of chains to count as your first stitch. (It isn't always necessary to tie a knot, but it's a good idea if you're using a slippery material or if there's a danger of the work coming apart.) On your sampler, join a new color yarn (Color B) onto the end of the last treble crochet row. Do 2 rows of single crochet with the new color.

To join a new yarn in the middle of the row, stop whatever stitch you're doing at the point where you have 2 loops on the hook. Complete the stitch with the new color, leaving a 3" end. Carry all loose ends along with your work to save time later.

Finishing with a Slip Stitch (sl st)

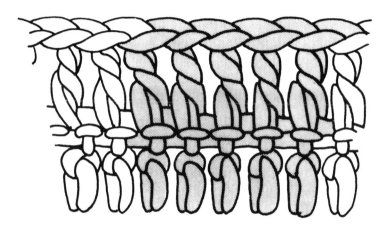

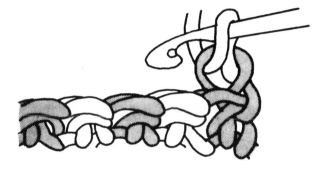

At the end of the last row of single crochet on your sampler, chain 3 and turn. Do 5 double crochet using Color B, join on the original color and do 5 more stitches, pick up Color B and do the remaining 5 stitches. Work a total of 5 rows in this manner, keeping the colors on top of each other to make vertical stripes.

Step 1. *Chain 1 at the end of the last row and turn.*

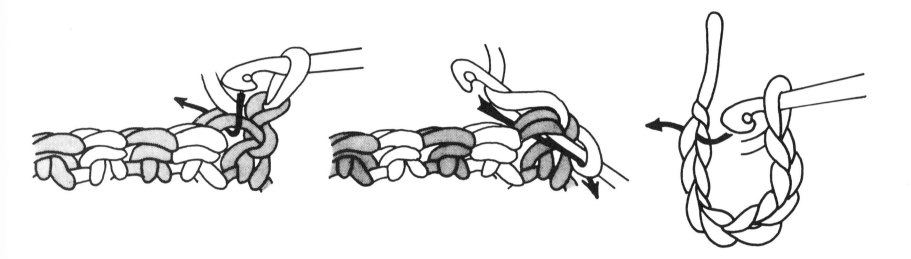

Step 2. *Insert the hook under both top pieces of the first stitch of the previous row.*

Step 3. *Yarn over. Pull the yarn through the stitch below* **and** *the loop on the hook in the direction of the arrow. There is now 1 loop on the hook and you've made 1 slip stitch. Continue making slip stitches loosely across the row for a neat edging.*

Step 1. *Chain 8 and insert the hook in the first chain in the direction of the arrow.*

Weaving in Loose Ends

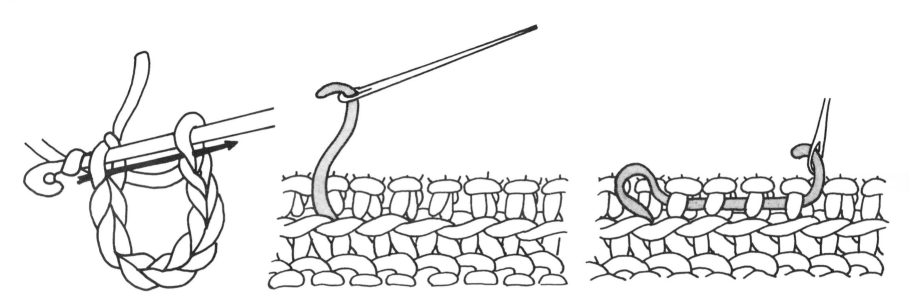

Step 2. *Yarn over. Pull the yarn through the chain **and** the loop on the hook in the direction of the arrow. There is now 1 loop on the hook and the ring is closed.*

Step 1. *Thread the loose end into a blunt-pointed yarn needle.*

Step 2. *Weave the end (the shaded yarn) into the back of your work, taking care to catch only the back pieces of the stitches. Finish off any ends left on your sampler. This makes a difference in how professional your work will look.*

4. Fancy Stitches

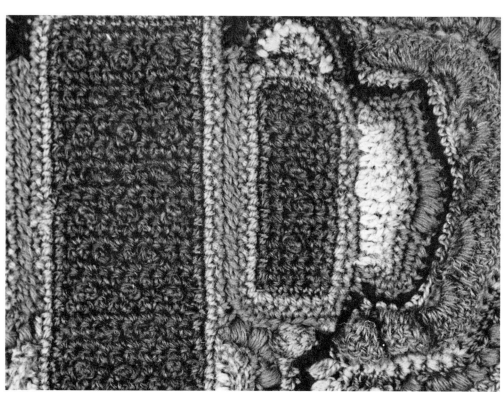

*A **Halter Top** (Left) by Susan Morrow. Susan used wool yarn and many fancy stitches to create a rich texture but still maintained a basically simple design. Can you identify the different stiches used in the detail above?*

No matter how complicated some fancy stitches might look, they're all combinations of stitches you've learned in the last chapter: chain stitch, single crochet, half-double crochet, double crochet, and treble crochet. There are hundreds of fancy stitches so we're going to show you a few of our favorites. It's not all that important to learn a multitude of these stitches out of context, but it is important to see how a few of them will work with others to give unusual effects within a given design. Sometimes these stitches are used to make an all-over design and sometimes they're used for accent. It all depends on what you're making. After you've mastered these fancy stitches, you can refer to the books that specialize in explaining many stitches—Mon Tricot's *1030 Stitches* is great.

Once again we're going to make samplers. They'll include shell stitch; filet pattern; variations of simple stitches with changing colors, picots and bar stitches; and accent stitches—popcorn stitch, cluster stitch, hazelnut stitch, bump stitch, and Judith stitch. These all produce interesting effects and will give you a good understanding of fancy stitches.

All the sampler directions at the end of this chapter are written in the usual "crochet language." This language is what you're up against if you want to use standard patterns. To make things a little easier, all the samplers are diagramed with symbols that we adapted from Japanese crochet patterns. They're a visual aid to the written directions, so, as you work, keep refering to them. We can't stress enough how important it is to think *visually* when you crochet: what effect will I get if I use this stitch? When you follow patterns it's very hard to do this because you get so hung up on words.

After you've made all four samplers, we're going to join them together to make a larger one. Then you'll learn edging with the tapestry stitch, open scallops, picots, and two stitches that give a corded effect: the shrimp stitch, and the Janet stitch. Since all the samplers are to be joined into a large rectangle, be sure to keep them each the same size. Even though the directions are geared so each sampler will be the same size, it doesn't hurt to keep this in mind.

Shell Stitch Sampler

The shell stitch consists of several doubles or trebles done in one stitch that makes a shape like a clam shell. There are many ways to do it, each one producing a different effect. In the sampler we'll use a basic shell stitch, a shell stitch between straight rows, a checkerboard effect, and zigzags. The shell stitch can also make a scalloped edge when done as the last row.

Filet Pattern Sampler

The filet pattern was originally used to make crocheted pictures, or picture lace, but can be adapted to any solid-color design that can be charted on graph paper. Basically it's a combination of solid blocks of crochet made with doubles, and open spaces made by skipping stitches and compensating with chains. It's good practice in the math of crochet (counting your stitches) because for every stitch you skip, you must make a chain. The filet pattern is great for openwork designs (a delicate vest, for example). And why not try weaving a

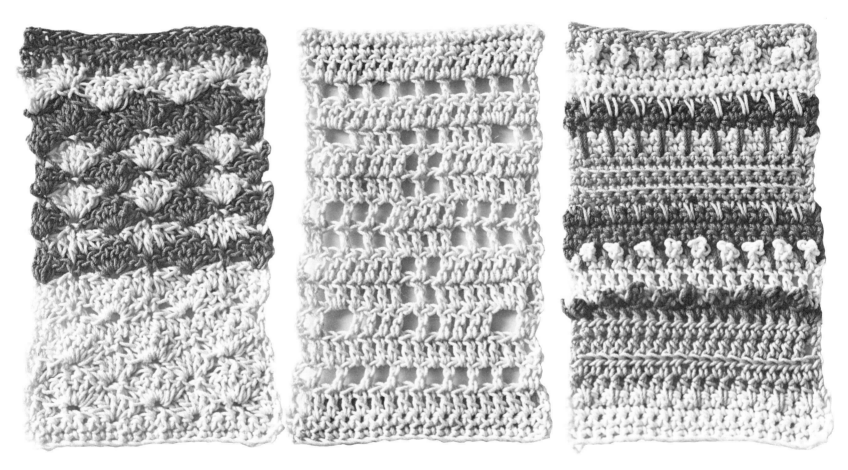

The Shell Stitch Sampler.

The Filet Pattern Sampler.

The Picot and Bar Stitch Sampler.

The Accent Stitch Sampler.

contrasting piece of ribbon through the spaces after the piece is done? It would look great in a hat.

Picot and Bar Stitch Sampler

Picots are little nubs made with chain stitches. Originally they were used only for edging, but they also work very well within a design.

Bar stitches are singles or half-doubles made by inserting your hook one or two rows below the row you're working on. They make a long stitch with a rich textural effect that really comes through if you use a contrasting color.

In this sampler we've combined both picots and bar stitches with simple stitches to give you several of the effects possible.

Accent Stitch Sampler

These stitches zap up your work and are really fun to do. The bump, Judith, and cluster stitches can be used as an all-over texture or as accent. The hazelnut and popcorn stitches are three-dimensional and usually used as accent. They also look great when done in a contrasting color.

Joining Two Pieces of Crochet

Now we'll join the finished samplers together to make one big piece. Like just about everything in crochet, there are several ways to do this. But before you can join anything together, the pieces must be edged all around in single crochet. This provides a neatly finished edge and also makes it much easier to join them. We'll forget about crochet language for now and explain the following techniques in plain English.

After you've got all four samplers edged, you're ready to join them together. You'll learn three methods for joining: slip stitch, single crochet, and sewing. Practice the three on scrap swatches before you decide which one you want to use. In our sampler we joined the pieces with single crochet on the right side of the work.

Border Stitches

When all four samplers are joined together, the next things to learn are some stitches and effects for borders around the edge.

The first is the *tapestry stitch*, which is single crochet used to simulate a tapestry, rug, or any multicolored design that can be charted on graph paper. Why not try adapting an old cross-stitch embroidery pattern sometime? Tapestry stitch works best in the round so that's why it makes such a good border stitch. We've done a very simple border using arrows and rectangles in two different colors on a light background.

The Completed Sampler of fancy stitches.

The Border Stitches of the sampler shown in detail.

The next border effect is the *openwork scallop*, which gives a lacy design that's reminiscent of the borders grandma painstakingly did around pillowcases and handkerchiefs. But using yarn instead of thread makes all the difference in how it looks. The variations on this effect are endless, but we've done a simple style of scallop that explains the basic technique.

One of the most effective ways to end a border in crochet is with a *corded edge*, which gives an almost beadlike effect that really finishes a piece off well. The two cord stitches are strange to do because they're the only stitches in crochet worked from left to right. But with a little practice, you'll get used to going backwards. The first cord stitch is the *shrimp stitch*, which is merely single crochet worked from left to right. The second cord stitch is the *Janet stitch*, a more decorative border made with a slip stitch and a chain.

This sampler will come in handy later on for reference. In fact, why not hang it on the wall for inspiration?

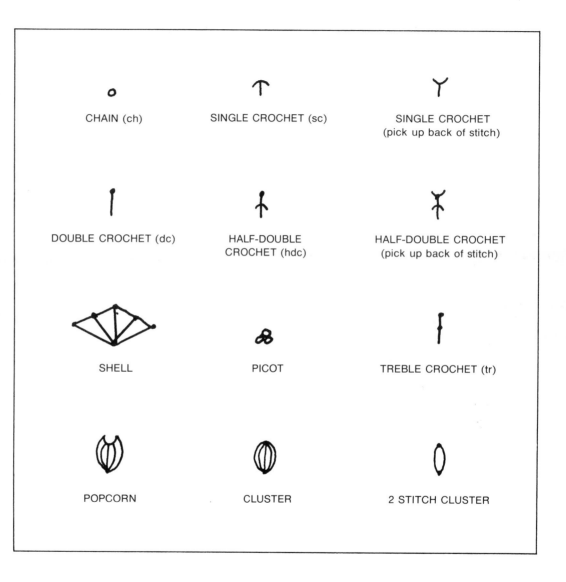

CHAIN (ch)

SINGLE CROCHET (sc)

SINGLE CROCHET
(pick up back of stitch)

DOUBLE CROCHET (dc)

HALF-DOUBLE
CROCHET (hdc)

HALF-DOUBLE CROCHET
(pick up back of stitch)

SHELL

PICOT

TREBLE CROCHET (tr)

POPCORN

CLUSTER

2 STITCH CLUSTER

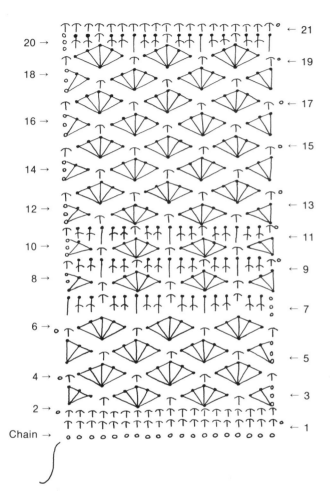

Shell Stitch Sampler

Foundation Chain—*ch 20 with color A.*

Row 1. *1 sc in 2nd ch from hook. Continue doing 1 sc in each ch across row (19 sts).*

Row 2. *Ch 1 and turn. Sc across row.*

Row 3. *Ch 3 and turn. 2 dc in 1st st (1 half shell made). Skip 2 sts. Sc in next st. *Skip 2 sts. 5 dc in next st. Skip 2 sts. Sc in next st (1 whole shell made).* Repeat from * to * 1 time. Skip 2 sts and do 3 dc in last st (1 half shell made).*

Row 4. *Ch 1 and turn. 1 sc in 1st st. Repeat from * to * (in row 3) 3 times (3 whole shells). Row should end with 1 sc.*

Row 5. *Repeat row 3.*

Row 6. *Repeat row 4.*

Row 7. *Ch 3 and turn. Making 1 st in each dc of the shell *1 hdc, 1 hdc, 1 sc, 1 hdc, 1 hdc, 1 dc.* Repeat from * to * 2 times. (Note how you've eliminated the scalloped effect).*

Row 8. *Repeat row 3 (this shell row brings back the scalloped effect).*

Row 9. *Ch 1 and turn. Making 1 st in each st * 1 sc, 1 hdc, 1 hdc, 1 dc, 1 hdc, 1 hdc*. Repeat from*

* to * 2 times. End row with 1 sc. Break off yarn.*

Row 10. *Attach color B. Repeat row 3. Break off yarn.*

Row 11. *Attach color A. Repeat row 9. Break off yarn.*

Row 12. *Attach color B. Repeat row 3. Break off yarn.*

Row 13. *Attach color A. Repeat row 4. Break off yarn.*

Row 14. *Attach color B. Repeat row 3. Break off yarn.*

Row 15. *Attach color A. Repeat row 4. Break off yarn.*

Row 16. *Attach color B. Repeat row 3 (Note the checkerboard effect).*

Row 17. *Repeat row 4. Break off yarn.*

Row 18. *Attach color A. Repeat row 3.*

Row 19. *Repeat row 4. Break off yarn (note the zig-zag effect).*

Row 20. *Attach color B. Repeat row 7.*

Row 21. *Sc across row. End off piece.*

Filet Pattern Sampler

Foundation Chain—ch 20.

Row 1. 1 sc in 2nd ch from hook. Continue doing 1 sc in each ch across row. (19 sts).

Row 2. Ch 1 and turn. Sc across row.

Row 3. Ch 3 and turn. Dc across row.

Row 4. Ch 3 and turn. *1 dc, ch 1, skip 1 st.* Repeat from * to * 7 times. 2 dc. (8 spaces made).

Row 5. Ch 3 and turn. Dc across row going into each st and each ch sp.

Row 6. Ch 3 and turn. 1 dc, ch 2, skip 2 sts, 4 dc, ch 1, skip 1 st, 1 dc, ch 1, skip 1 st, 4 dc, ch 2, skip 2 sts, 2 dc (2 big sps and 2 small sps made).

Row 7. Ch 3 and turn. 1 dc, 2 dc in ch 2 sp, 4 dc, ch 1, skip ch sp, 1 dc, ch 1, skip ch sp, 4 dc, 2 dc in ch 2 sp, 2 dc (2 sps made).

Row 8. Ch 3 and turn. 7 dc, ch 1, skip ch 1 sp, 1 dc, ch 1, skip ch 1 sp, 8 dc (2 sps made).

Row 9. Ch 3 and turn. * 1 dc, ch 1, skip 1 st, 1 dc.* Repeat from * to * 2 times. 1 dc in ch 1 sp, 1 dc, 1 dc in ch 1 sp. Repeat from * to * 3 times. End row with 1 dc (6 sps made).

Row 10. Ch 3 and turn. Repeat row 9 doing dc over dc and sps over sps (6 sps made).

Row 11. (From now on it's up to you to make the right number of turning chains—we're not going to mention it anymore). Same as row 7 but remember to do 1 st in every st and 1 st in every ch sp. Remember this in the following rows.

Row 12. Repeat row 11.

Row 13. Repeat row 6.

Row 14. Dc across row.

Row 15. Repeat row 4.

Row 16. Dc across row.

Row 17. Sc across row.

Row 18. Sc across row. End off piece.

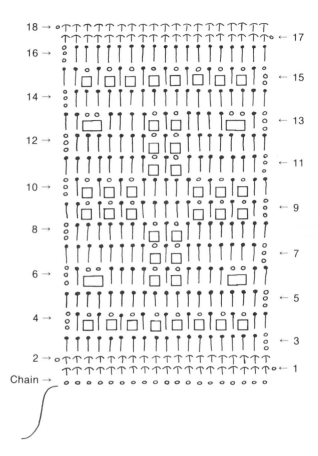

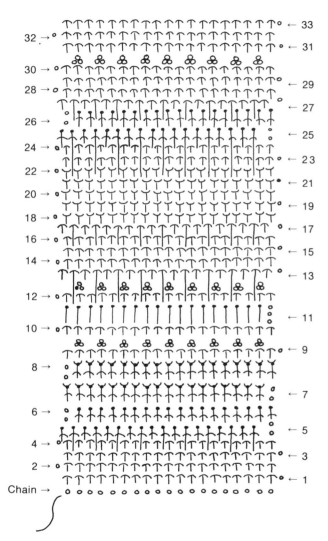

Simple Stitches, Picots, and Bar Stitch Sampler

Foundation Chain—ch 20.

Row 1. Using color A, sc across row (19 sts).

Row 2. Sc across row.

Row 3. Sc across row.

Row 4. Sc across row. Break off yarn.

Row 5. Attach color B. *1 hdc in st one row below (1 hdc bar st made), 1 hdc in next st*. Repeat from * to * 8 times.

Row 6. Hdc across row.

Row 7. Hdc across row picking up back piece of each st.

Row 8. Repeat row 7. Break off yarn.

Row 9. Attach color C. *2 sc, ch 3, sl st into front piece of 2nd sc (1 picot made). Repeat from * to * 8 times. End row with 1 sc. Break off yarn.

Row 10. Attach color A. Sc across row pushing picots to right side of work.

Row 11. Dc across row.

Row 12. * Sc, 1 sc with a picot * Repeat from * to * 8 times (9 picots altogether). End with 1 sc. Break off yarn.

Row 13. Attach color C. * 1 sc, 1 sc bar st dropped below picot row (to left of picot)*. Repeat from * to * 8 times. End row with 1 sc.

Row 14. Sc across row.

Row 15. Sc across row.

Row 16. Sc across row. Break off yarn.

Row 17. Attach color B. *1 sc, 1 sc bar st*. Repeat from * to * 8 times. End row with 1 sc.

Row 18. Sc across row picking up back piece of each st.

Row 19. Repeat row 18.

Row 20. Repeat row 18.

Row 21. Repeat row 18.

Row 22. Repeat row 18. Break off yarn.

Row 23. Attach color A. Sc across row.

Row 24. Sc across row. Break off yarn.

Row 25. Attach color C. * 1 hdc bar st dropped down 3 rows (hits color B), 1 hdc*. Repeat from * to * 8 times. End row with 1 hdc.

Row 26. Hdc across row. Break off yarn.

Row 27. Attach color A. *1 sc, 1 sc bar st*. Repeat from * to * 8 times. End row with 1 sc.

Row 28. Sc across row.

Row 29. Sc across row.

Row 30. Repeat row 12. Break off yarn.

Row 31. Attach color B. Sc across row.

Row 32. Repeat row 31.

Row 33. Repeat row 31. End off piece.

Accent Stitch Sampler

Foundation Chain—ch 20 with color A.

Row 1. *Sc across row (19 sts).*

Row 2. *Sc across row.*

Row 3. *Sc across row.*

Row 4. * *1 sc, 1 tr** (**bump st** *made by alternating 1 sc and 1 tr. It's done on wrong side of work so trs form bumps which pop out on right side). Repeat from * to * 8 times. End row with 1 sc.*

Row 5. *Sc across row.*

Row 6. *Repeat row 4 (bump st).*

Row 7. *Sc across row. Break off yarn.*

Row 8. *Attach color B. Sc across row.*

Row 9. *2 dc, 1* **popcorn st** *(5 dc in 1 st, remove hook, insert into 1st of the 5 dc, pick up dropped loop and pull it through, ch 1) *3 dc, 1 popcorn st *. Repeat from * to * 2 times. End row with 3 dc (there are 4 popcorns in row).*

Row 10. *Sc across row. (Remember to count your sts. A popcorn is only* **one** *st.)*

Row 11. *4 dc, 1 popcorn, 3 dc, 1 popcorn, 3 dc, 1 popcorn, 5 dc (3 popcorns in row).*

Row 12. *Sc across row. Break off yarn.*

Row 13. *Attach color C. 1 dc, 1* **judith st*** *(skip 1 st, 3 dc in next 3 sts. With hook in front of the 3 dc, insert in skipped st. Pull a long loop through, yo, and pull through 2 loops)* Repeat from * to * 3 times. End row with 1 dc.*

Row 14. *Sc across row.*

Row 15. *Repeat row 13.*

Row 16. *Sc across row.*

Row 17. *Repeat row 13. Break off yarn.*

Row 18. *Attach color B. Sc across row.*

Row 19. *3 sc, 1* **hazelnut st** *(*yo, insert hook into next st, yo, pull through 1 loop, yo, pull through 2 loops*. Repeat from * to * 5 times in the* **same** *st. Yo, pull through all 6 loops on hook. Ch 1). *3 sc, 1 hazelnut*. Repeat from * to * 2 times. End row with 1 sc.*

Row 20. *Sc across row (Remember a hazelnut is only* **one** *st).*

Row 21. *1 sc, 1 hazelnut, *3 sc, complete 3rd sc with color C, 1 hazelnut in color C making final ch with color B*. Repeat from * to * 2 times, carrying the unused color along. In color B, 3 sc, 1 hazelnut.*

Row 22. *Sc across row.*

Row 23. *Repeat row 19.*

Row 24. *Sc across row. Break off yarn.*

Row 25. *Attach color A. Ch 3, 1* **cluster st** *(start dc in next st until there are 2 loops on hook, start another dc in same st, work loops off 2 by 2). 1 cluster st in each st across row.*

Row. 26. *Sc across row.*

Row 27. *Repeat row 25.*

Row 28. *Sc across row. End off piece.*

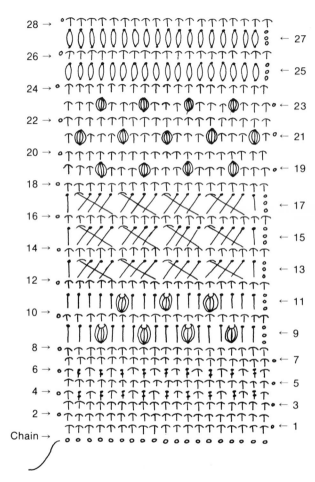

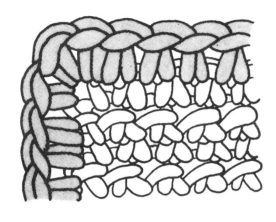

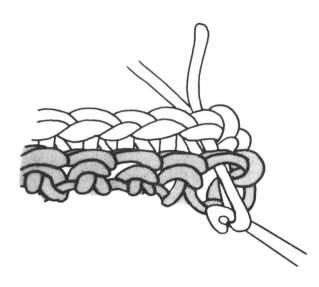

Step 1. *Take one of your samplers and join whatever color you like onto the right-hand side of the top edge (we used the cream). Chain 2. Note that whenever you work in the round with single crochet, your chain 2 counts as the first stitch. This makes it easier to spot where the round begins. Instead of working in a spiral, each round is joined, the appropriate number of chains made, and the next round started.*

Step 2. *Make 2 singles in the same stitch. This becomes your corner.*

Step 3. *Single crochet along the top of the piece. When you come to the last stitch, do 3 singles into it to turn the corner.*

Step 4. *Edging down the vertical edge of a piece of crochet is a matter of feel. Usually you do 1 single in each row of singles. In doubles you do 2 or 3. Feel your way down the edge and find the neatest way for you.*

Step 5. *When you get to the end of the edge, do 3 singles in the last stitch.*

Step 6. *Continue with singles until you get back to the first chain 2. Slip stitch into the top chain to close the round.*

Step 7. *Chain 2 and do another round of edging, making sure to do 3 singles in each corner. Join the second round with a slip stitch then break off and secure the yarn.*

Slip Stitch Method. Step 1. *First lay the 2 pieces together with the right sides facing each other. Then attach the joining yarn and pull a loop through.*

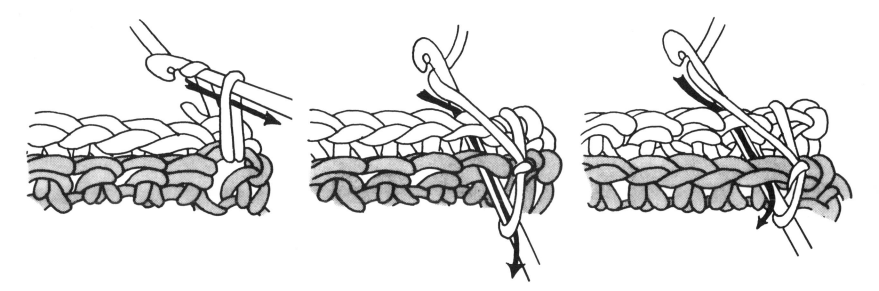

Step 2. *Yarn over and pull the yarn through in the direction of the arrow. Hold onto the loose end to make sure it doesn't slip through.*

Step 3. *Insert the hook through the tops of both stitches, yarn over, and pull the yarn through the loop in the direction of the arrow. This makes 1 slip stitch. When you join with slip stitches it's very important to keep the stitches loose so the work dosen't buckle. Continue the join, matching stitch for stitch. At the end of the piece, break off the yarn and secure it.*

Single Crochet Method. Step 1. *First lay the 2 pieces together with the wrong sides facing each other. This will make the join show on the right side. (For a different effect, you can also try it on the wrong side.) Now attach the joining yarn in the same way as the slip stitch method and pull a loop through in the direction of the arrow.*

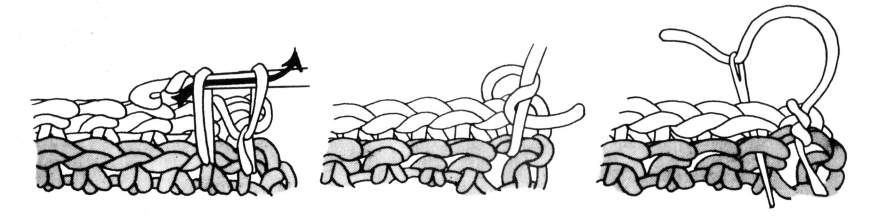

Step 2. *Yarn over and pull the yarn through the 2 loops in the direction of the arrow. You've made 1 single crochet joining stitch. This method also works when you pick up only the inside pices of each stitch, giving you a ridge on either side of the join. Continue the join, matching stitch for stitch. At the end of the piece, break off the yarn and secure it.*

Sewing Method. Step 1. *Lay the 2 pieces together with the right sides facing each other. Thread a length of yarn through a blunt-pointed yarn needle. Now insert the needle through both first stitches and tie a knot.*

Step 2. *Catching both pieces of each stitch, sew the pieces together with an overhand whip stitch. This means that the needle will always be inserted in the same direction (in our example it's from back to front). Continue the join, matching stitch for stitch. Be sure not to pull the yarn too tight. At the end of the join make several overhand stitches on top of each other, secure them with a knot, and break off the yarn.*

Tapestry Stitch

Step 1. *Join the background color onto a corner of your large sampler. Chain 2 and single crochet until you want to start an arrow.*

Step 2. *Join on color B and do 3 singles, completing the last one with color A. Then continue with singles until you want to make a rectangle.*

Step 3. *Drop color A and join on color C. Do 3 singles, completing the last one in color A.*

Step 4. *Continue around the whole piece until you get back to the first chain 2. Slip stitch into the top chain, chain 2 again, and follow the charted design for the second round. (As with simple edging, you don't work in a spiral—each round is closed with a slip stitch, the appropriate number of chains made, and the next round started.) There are 9 rounds of tapestry stitch bordering the sampler. Break off the yarn when you're done. The trickiest thing about this stitch is carrying along the color(s) not in use. Just before you drop a color, give the yarn a little tug to make sure it's lying flat. Also make sure to do 3 singles in each corner to keep the piece from buckling.*

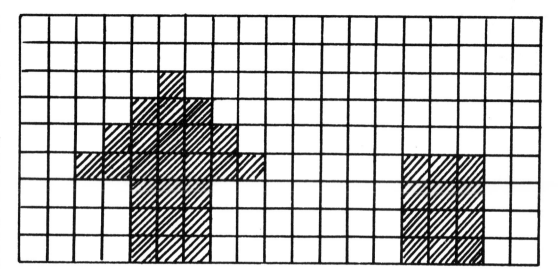

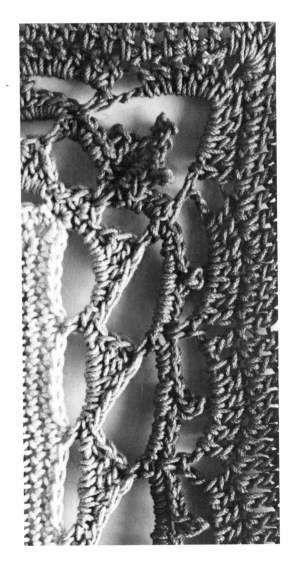

Openwork Scallops

Round 1. Step 1. *Join on any color you like in the center stitch of any corner. Chain 2 and do 2 singles in the same stitch. (Corner increase, remember?)*

Step 2. *Chain 5 and single into the 6th stitch. Continue with the 5 chains and single in the 6th stitch around the whole sampler. If you want the scallops to be spaced perfectly, count the number of stitches on each side of the sampler and find the closest number that divides into it. Say you have 48 stitches—then the scallops would be made to cover 6 stitches 8 times. If you don't have an exact division, juggle the skipped stitches so it's not too obvious. Even if you don't space them exactly, it's important to remember to do 3 singles in each corner.*

Step 3. *When you get back to the first chain 2, slip stitch into the top chain to close the first round.*

Round 2. Step 1. *Chain 2 and do 2 singles in the middle single of the round below. You're ready to make the scallops.*

Step 2. *Into the loop of each chain 5 do 1 single, 1 half-double, 1 double, 1 treble, 1 double, 1 half-double, and 1 single.*

Step 3. *Skip the single from the previous round and continue making a scallop in each loop of chains. When you get a corner do 3 singles into the center single of the previous round.*

Step 4. *At the end of the round, slip stitch into the top chain of the first chain 2. Break off the yarn.*

Round 3. Step 1. *Join another color onto the center single in one of the corners. Chain 2 for the first stitch, chain 5, and do another single in the center stitch. Then chain 4 and do a single in the treble from the previous round (the center of the scallop).*

Step 2. *Chain 6 and do a single into the treble of the next scallop. Continue in this way until you've made a single in the last scallop before a corner.*

Step 3. *Chain 4, do a single into the center stitch, chain 5, single into the same stitch, chain 4, and do a single into the treble of the next scallop. Continue with Step 2 until you come to the next corner. Then repeat Step 3.*

Step 4. *When you get back to the first chain 2, slip stitch into the top chain to close the round.*

Round 4. Step 1. *Now we're going to make scallops with picots in the center. Slip stitch into the chain 5 at the corner (this puts you in position to start the scallop), chain 2 for the first stitch, and make 1 single with a picot on it. Do 5 singles into the chain loop with a picot on every other stitch (there should be 3 picots). Do 4 singles into the next chain loop. This completes the first corner.*

Step 2. *In the next chain loop do 4 singles, 1 single with a picot, and 4 more singles. Continue around the sampler until you get to the chain loop before the corner.*

Step 3. *Do 4 singles in this chain loop, then make 6 singles with a picot on every other stitch. Do 4 singles in the next chain loop and continue until you get to the next corner. Then repeat Step 2.*

Step 4. *Continue around the sampler and join with a slip stitch when you get to the end of the round. Break off the yarn.*

Round 5. Step 1. *Now we're going to bring the border back to a rectangle. Join the same color on to any of the spaces between the scallops. Chain 2 for the first stitch and then chain 8. Do 1 single in the space between the scallops of the previous round.*

Step 2. *Continue around the sampler until you get to the last scallop before a corner. Chain 10, going right over the 3-picot scallop, do 1 single into the space between the next 2 scallops, and continue as above.*

Step 3. *At the end of the round, slip stitch into the first chain 2.*

Round 6. Step 1. *Slip stitch into the next chain loop, chain 3, and do 6 doubles into the same chain loop. Skip over the single from the previous round and do 7 doubles into the next chain loop.*

Step 2. *Continue around the sampler, doing 11 doubles in each corner.*

Step 3. *At the end of the round, slip stitch into the top chain of the first chain 3.*

Round 7. Step 1. *Chain 3 and do 1 double in each double of the previous round.*

Step 2. *Do 4 doubles in each corner. At the end of the round, slip stitch to join, and break off the yarn. The border should now be back to a rectangular shape.*

Corded Edges

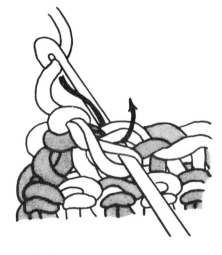

Shrimp Stitch. Step 1. *Join a contrasting color onto the long end of the sampler on the left side. Chain 1 and insert the hook into the next stitch **to the right** in the direction of the arrow.*

Step 2. *Pull a loop through in the direction of the arrow.*

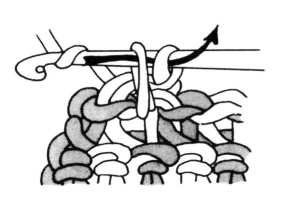

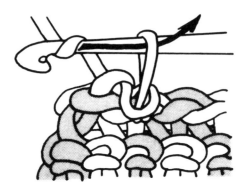

Step 3. *Yarn over and pull the yarn through in the direction of the arrow. This completes 1 shrimp stitch, which is the same as a single crochet only it's done from left to right.*

Step 4. *Continue doing the shrimp stitch until you get to the right hand side of the sampler.*

Janet Stitch. Step 1. *Insert the hook into the next stitch to the right and pull the yarn through in the direction of the arrow. This is the same as a slip stitch only it's done from left to right.*

Step 2. *Make 1 chain.*

Step 3. *Repeat Steps 1 and 2 until you reach the right-hand side of the border. Do a row of shrimp stitch on the next long edge and finish up the sampler with a row of Janet stitch on the other short edge. Slip stitch into the first shrimp stitch, secure the yarn, and that's it.*

A Child's Cape by Joan Wortis. With its contrasting colors and rich textures, this cape, made of wool and chenille, is a wearable sampler of fancy stitches.

Wool Hat (Left) by Sharron Hedges. Besides its unusual shape, what makes this hat special is the rich texture created by the hazelnut stitches spaced close together. Note the shrimp stitch edge at the bottom and the delicate sea shells worked in at the top.

Crazy Quilt Afghan (Right) by Helen Bitar. No two areas are alike in this wild design made with wool yarn. Helen has used every stitch and motif she could think of. Known for her brightly colored stitchery, Helen has just begun experimenting with crochet. Photo by Helen Bitar.

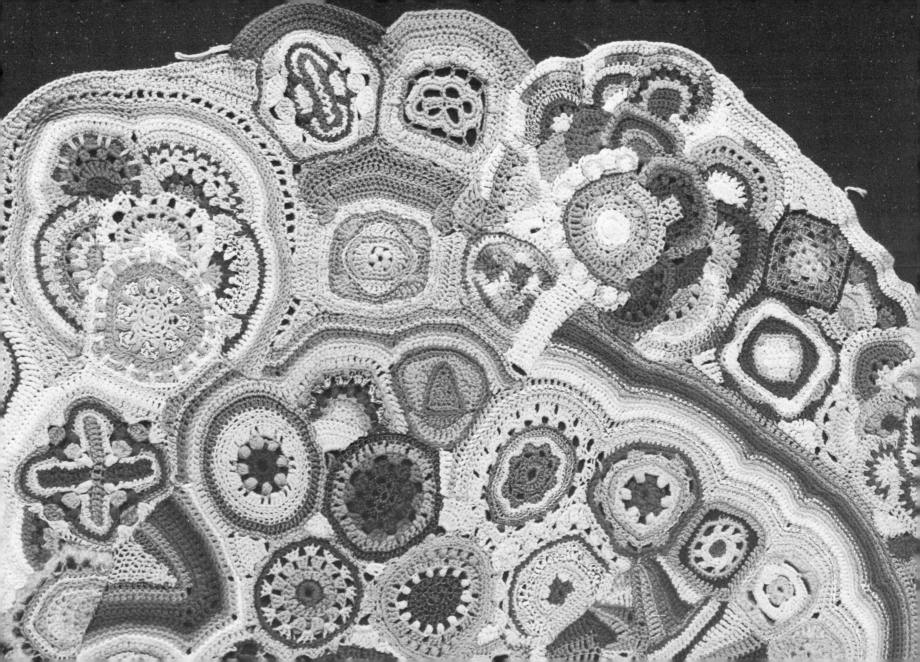

5. Shapes

Geometric Pillow Cover (Above) by Paulette Stammer. This simple, high-contrast design was worked from the center out in wool yarn.

Vest (Right) by Cindy Picchi. This design also grows from the center. Note the ovals on either side and the modified diamond shape in the center.

All the work done up to now has been in rows going back and forth, which is how most traditional crochet is done. But we're interested in getting away from the traditional—in a way, it's like creating a whole new craft. Most of the finished work in this book was made by combining shapes rather than repeating rows, and this is the most important concept of all to deal with. Just like the samplers you've already done, making shapes is a simple, logical process based on understanding and applying certain techniques.

This chapter will show you how to make a variety of shapes and then put them all together in a pillow sampler. The technique for each shape discussed, as well as the pillow sampler, is demonstrated at the end of the chapter. The pillow sampler will give you the basic knowledge in using shapes that you'll need to build any design you want. It may be a little tricky at first, but with practice and ripping out you'll get a feel for it. If you can make these basic shapes then everything that follows—fitting clothes, making free designs, geometric shapes—will be a breeze.

The most widely used techniques for making shapes are increasing and decreasing. Increasing makes the work wider by adding stitches, decreasing makes it narrower by eliminating stitches. By combining the two you can make all kinds of interesting shapes.

Basic Shapes

We'll start with some of the most basic shapes, and from there you can experiment with your own. You'll notice in the demonstrations that all the directions call for single crochet. This is because single defines the shapes well without making them floppy. You could use half-double or double as well, because decreasing and increasing are the same no matter what stitch you use.

Spool Shape. The spool shape is a good one to start with because it depends on both increasing and decreasing to give it shape.

Triangles and Diamonds. Triangles are wonderful shapes—they can be used alone or combined to make stars, diamonds, etc. If you want to crochet a triangle starting at the base (the wide part), you decrease until you reach the point. If you want to start at the point, you increase until the base becomes the width you want. A natural extension of the triangle is the diamond. To make it, you'll crochet a triangle starting at the point, work up to the base, and decrease back down to the point.

Circle. The next shape shown will be the circle. Circles are very simple once you understand the concept of increasing in the round. The same increase pattern holds true no matter what stitch you work a circle in. After you try a circle in single crochet, try one in double also.

Square. You already know how to make the simplest kind of square—just crochet a row of singles and then make the same number of rows as stitches. Starting a square in the center, however, is similar to making a circle in the round and gives a different effect than just crocheting rows back and forth.

Oval. The last of the basic shapes is the oval. There are two ways to make ovals: the first is long and skinny and the second is more rounded. The demonstration will show you both ways.

Unusual Shapes

There are several fancy shapes in crochet that are fun to do and bound to get your imagination going. With these more unusual shapes, it's a good idea to draw a picture of the shape first, then use the picture as your directions instead of words. This will help you to think visually in terms of shape and design. The two shapes we want to consider are fingers and the snail.

Fingers. These are just what they sound like—finger-shaped pieces worked off another piece of crochet. They're very simple and can be effective in an all-over design or as an accent. We will do them in four different colors so you can see how they grow.

Snail. Now draw a picture of a snail, and try and imagine how you would crochet it. We'll do it two different ways—starting at the long end and starting at the center.

Pillow Sampler

As you crochet more, certain techniques will become favorites—you'll find yourself combining colors and shapes in ways that are very personal and unique. The pillow sampler demonstrated is the most ambitious one so far because it shows some of the many ways shapes can be added to shapes to form a design. And this is the most advanced step in crochet. Making this sampler will give you some real ideas to work with, and hopefully you'll go on to designs of your own. Also, this is the most loosely-written of all the samplers so far; no more step-by-step directions. You will know how to make all the basic shapes, but refer back to the shape demonstrations if you have to.

Use yarn that you really like for this sampler. You'll need 5 colors, material for backing (we used suede), and stuffing. The photos show you each step in the growth of the design—an incredibly organic process.

Spool Shape

First Decrease Method. Step 1. *Make a foundation chain of 16 chains and do 1 row of singles (15 stitches).*

Step 2. *Chain 1 and turn. Do 1 single, skip the next stitch and continue across the row. The skipped stitch is 1 decrease, and you should now have 14 stitches.*

Step 3. *Chain 1 and turn. Do 1 single, do 1 decrease, and continue across the row. You should now have 13 stitches.*

Step 2. *Yarn over and pull through all 3 loops.*

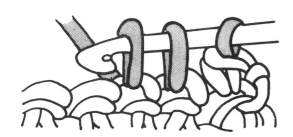

Second Decrease Method. Step 1. *There is another way to decrease that doesn't leave a hole. Think of it as combining 2 stitches to make 1. Start a single crochet, stop when you have 2 loops on the hook. Start another single in the next stitch—you should now have 3 loops on the hook.*

Step 3. *You have turned 2 stitches into 1, therefore 1 decrease is made. This method works the same with half-double, double, and treble, and is much neater than a skipped stitch.*

Back to the Spool Shape.

Step 4. *Do 1 single, 1 decrease as explained and continue across the row.*

Step 5. *Continue decreasing in the second stitch of each row until you're down to 3 stitches.*

Step 6. *Now you're ready to slope outward. Do 1 single in the first stitch, do 2 singles in the second stitch (1 increase made). Continue with singles across the row.*

Step 7. *Continue doing 2 stitches in the second stitch of every row until you're back up to 15 stitches. Note that you've been increasing and decreasing in the second stitch from the edge of each row. This keeps the edge even and is easier to work off of.*

Step 8. *You'll notice that the edges of the shape are pretty ragged. It always looks better if you work a row of singles around the edge of the whole shape to give a good straight line. We did this in Chapter 4 and the only difference with the more elaborate shapes is that you must remember to decrease on the inside angle and increase on the outside angle. The photo shows the spool shape edged on the left side only.*

Triangles and Diamonds

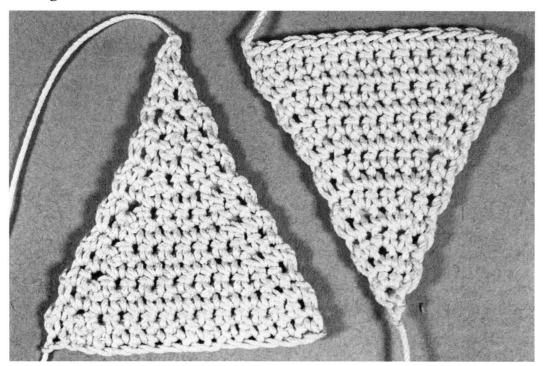 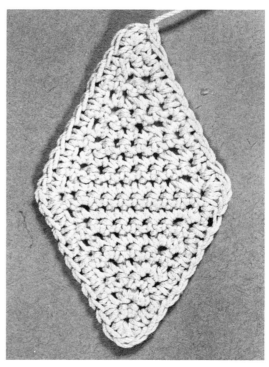

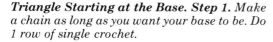

Triangle Starting at the Base. Step 1. *Make a chain as long as you want your base to be. Do 1 row of single crochet.*

Step 2. *Do 1 single in the first stitch, 1 decrease in the next stitch, and continue across the row.*

Step 3. *Continue decreasing in the second stitch of each row until you're down to 1 stitch, which is the point of the triangle.*

Triangle Starting at the Point. Step 1. *Chain 2 and make 1 single into the second chain.*

Step 2. *Chain 1 and turn. Do 3 singles into the 1 stitch.*

Step 3. *Do 1 single, make 1 increase in the second stitch and continue across the row.*

Step 4. *Continue making 1 increase in the second stitch of every row until the base is the length you want it.*

Diamond. *If you want to make a diamond, first make a triangle starting from a point. Then just start decreasing and sloping the edges up until you reach a point again.*

Circle

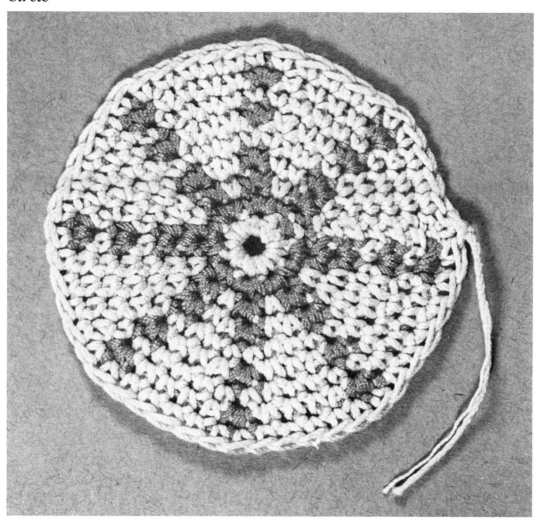

Step 1. *Chain 5 and join with a slip stitch to form a ring. Note that all the increases in the photo of the circle were done in darker yarn so you can see them better. You make it all one color.*

Round 1. *Chain 2 (the first stitch) and do 7 singles into the ring. Close the round with a slip stitch into the top chain of the first chain 2. You've made 8 singles into the ring.*

Round 2. *Chain 2 and make 2 stitches in each stitch. This will give you 16 stitches altogether.*

Round 3. *On the next round, do 1 increase every other stitch. This gives you 24 stitches.*

Round 4. *When you get to 24 stitches it's the time for the general circle concept to come into play. Think of the circle as 12 equal parts. Divide 24 stitches by 12 parts and you get 2. This means that you increase every second stitch on the next round.*

Round 5. *Then you do a round without increasing at all. This keeps the edge round and the circle flat.*

Round 6. *You now have 36 stitches, and 36 divided by 12 is 3, so you increase every third stitch. This goes on and on until the circle is the desired size. Don't forget to do a regular round without increases in between every increase round.*

If you want to do a huge circle, say for a rug, and you don't want to count every time you have to increase, you can do it visually. After your regular (non-increase) round, look down to the round below and you can see where you've increased (it looks like a vee). Do an increase on top of the second stitch of the increase from the last increase round. This way you can go on and on to make a room-sized rug.

Squares

Ovals

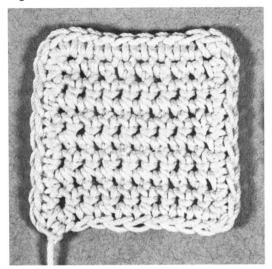

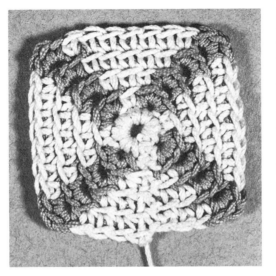

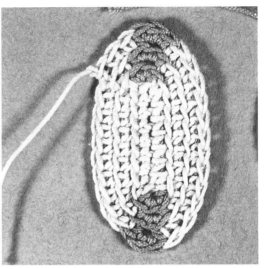

Square Worked in Rows. *This is the easiest type of square to do. Here we've done the square as 9 stitches by 9 rows. Then it was edged all around in single crochet.*

Square Started in the Center. Round 1. *Chain 5 and join with a slip stitch to form a ring. Note that the increases in the photo were done with a darker yarn so you could see them better. You make it all one color.*

Round 2. *Chain 2, then do 7 single crochet into the ring. Join with a slip stitch.*

Round 3. *Chain 2, do 3 singles in the next stitch, do 1 single, and do 3 singles in the next stitch. Repeat this 2 more times, so that each 3 singles makes a corner of the square.*

Round 4. *Chain 2, then do 1 single in each stitch until you come to a corner (the middle single from the last round). Do 3 singles in each center stitch to keep the corners sharp. Join each round with a slip stitch.*

Long and Skinny Oval. Round 1. *Make 10 chains. Do 1 row of single crochet. When you get to the last stitch of the row, do 3 singles in it. Then go back on the bottom of the foundation chain. When you get to the first stitch, do 3 singles into it. Join with a slip stitch.*

Round 2. *Chain 2 and do single crochet until you get to the increase from the first round. Do 3 singles in the center single, continue around the shape until you reach the next center. Do 3 singles in this stitch and then join with a slip stitch.*

Round 3. *Continue increasing at each end of the oval until it's reached the desired size. This method is best for small ovals, because if you keep adding onto it, it tends to become a circle.*

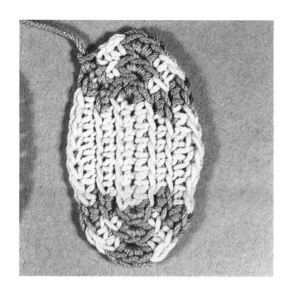

Fingers

Fat and Round Oval. Round 1. *Repeat Step 1 of the first method for making an oval.*

Round 2. *On the second round, increase 1 stitch before you reach the increase of the previous round. Do 1 single and then make 3 singles in the center stitch. Do 1 single and then increase 1 stitch. Continue with single until you reach the stitch before the increase on the other end. Then repeat the process.*

Round 3. *On the next round, keep the increase pattern going. But to make the oval fuller, do a few half-doubles on the top and bottom of the shape. This oval will remain an oval no matter how big you make it.*

Step 1. *Make a foundation chain of 29 chains in Color A.*

Step 2. *Do 7 singles. Then chain 7 and single crochet down like on a foundation chain. Do 7 singles off the original chain, chain 7, and single crochet down it. Do this once more and you'll have 3 fingers sticking up off the foundation chain.*

Step 3. *Join on Color B. Single crochet until you get to the base of a finger, skip 1 stitch (1 decrease) and single up the side. Do 3 singles in the point and then single down the other side. Decrease 1 stitch at the base of the finger, single until you come to the next finger, and repeat the above twice.*

Step 4. *Join on Color C and edge around each finger. Make sure to decrease 1 stitch on each side of the base and increase 1 stitch on either side of the point.*

Step 5. *Join on Color D. Edge around each finger, decreasing at each base and increasing at each side of the point.*

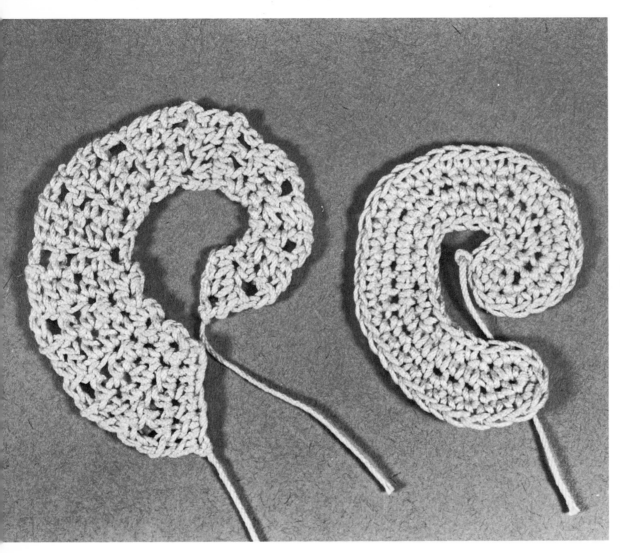

Snail Shape

Starting at Base. Step 1. *Make 7 chains for the foundation. Do 2 singles, 2 half-doubles and 2 doubles.*

Step 2. *Chain 3 and turn. Do 1 double, 2 half-doubles and 2 singles. Chain 1 and turn.*

Step 3. *Continue in this manner until you get to the ninth row. Then decrease 1 stitch on alternate sides every row. This will cause the shape to narrow out.*

Step 4. *Continue decreasing until you're down to 3 stitches, 1 single, 1 half-double and 1 double. This completes the shape.*

Starting in the Middle. Round 1. *Make a foundation chain about the size you want the finished shaped to be. Increase on one side of the chain about every third stitch on the beginning and every seventh at the tail. On the other side of the chain, decrease opposite the increase. This will make the shape curl a lot on one end but not so much on the other.*

Round 2. *Increase and decrease in the same way, making sure the increases and decreases aren't right on top of each other or it will turn the round edges into corners.*

Pillow Sampler

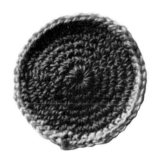

Step 1. *Make a circle about 2½" in diameter in color A.*

Step 2. *Edge the circle with round of Color B.*

Step 3. *Make squares around the circle in Color C. Here you have to do a little calculating. Count the stitches in the last row. We had 48 stitches, which gave us 6 squares each 8 stitches wide. Make each square, counting the left-hand edging as 1 stitch (7 stitches plus edge equals 8 stitches.) Continue around the circle with squares.*

Step 4. *Edge around all the squares with Color B. Remember to decrease where the squares come together (inside angles).*

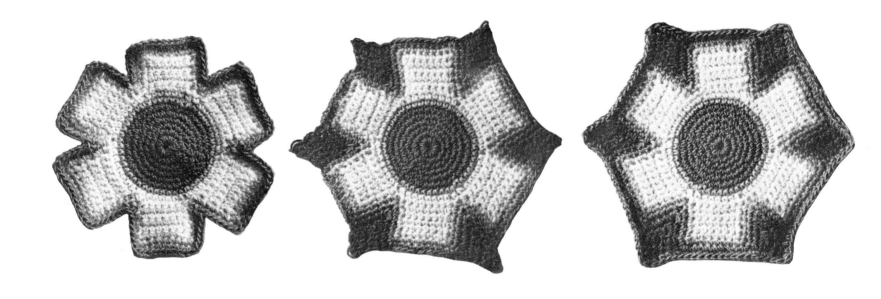

Step 5. *Edge around all the squares again using Color D. Remember that to keep the squares from buckling you must increase at the outside corners and decrease at the inside.*

Step 6. *Now fill in the spaces between the squares with diamonds in Color E. Using single crochet, begin at the corner of a square, go down the left side, and skip stitches (anywhere from 1-3 stitches) to keep everything flat. Then go up the right side of the next square. Make your turning chain and do a second row. Don't increase or decrease at the ends of these rows— the decrease at the inside angle will automatically form a diamond. Do 1 diamond in each space between the squares.*

Step 7. *Edge around the whole shape with a round of Color D.*

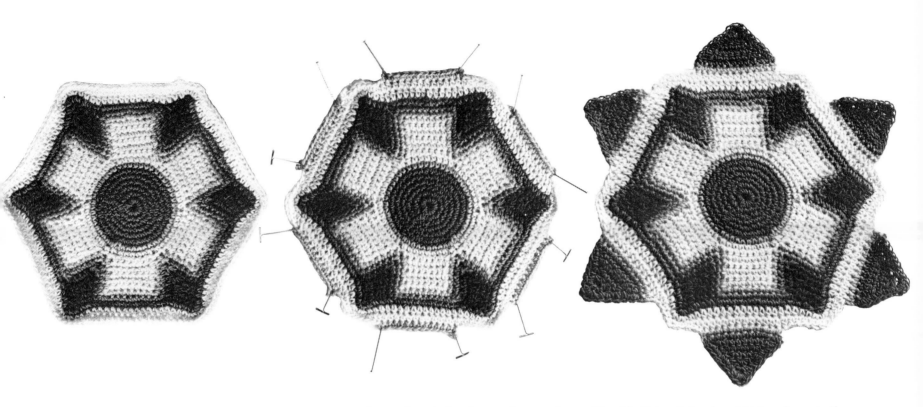

Step 8. *In Color C, edge around the outside using singles at the points and half-doubles between the points to fill in the dips. Do 2 or 3 rounds until you've got a nice even hexagon.*

Step 9. *Count the stitches from point to point. On our sampler there were 23 stitches on each face of the hexagon. In order to center the triangles that come next, we made them 13 stitches at the base. To start these triangles, do 13 stitches in Color B on all 6 sides.*

Step 10. *Using Color A, add triangles onto the stitches made in Step 9. Do 11 stitches beginning in the second stitch, so there's room for the edges around each triangle (Step 11).*

Step 11. *Attach Color B to the first stitch of the base from Step 9. Edge around each triangle, breaking off the yarn at the end of each one.*

Step 12. *Edge in Color C as you did in Step 8, with singles in the hills and half-doubles in the valleys. It will eventually give you a good even shape. Here we did 3 rounds in Color C, 1 round of all single with Color E, then 2 rounds in Color C with singles and half-doubles. Watch carefully as you go around so that you keep the piece flat.*

Making the Pillow

Now you've completed your beautiful design, so the next step is to make it into a pillow. First trace the outline of the crocheted piece right side up onto any material wrong side up that you want for the backing. We used suede because of its strength and softness. Whether you use leather or material, follow one of the methods for edging given in Chapter 9. Then crochet several rounds on the backing. Matching the wrong sides together, crochet around both the sampler and the backing. The corded edges described in Chapter 4 work especially well for this. If the pillow is to be a standard shape, you can buy a ready made one to stuff inside. If it's an unusual shape you can make a muslin-covered one yourself. Or, if the crocheted part is tightly made (no holes) like the one we did, you can stuff dacron or kapok right between the cover and the backing. Crochet around the pillow leaving just enough room so you can reach into the farthest corner with the stuffing. Then close up the opening and you have a finished pillow. If you're using a muslin pillow within the pillow, leave a big enough opening so you can stuff the pillow inside, then crochet the opening.

Arrow Vest (Front) by Sharron Hedges. This wool vest was built entirely of variations on the arrow shape. It was started with the star in the center and worked outwards.

Arrow Vest (Back) The arrows on the yoke are a continuation of the epaulets on the front. Note the beautiful shaping of the armhole.

Geometric Pillow Cover by Paulette Stammer. *This design, in wool yarn, shows what you can do with simple shapes—circles, fingers, and triangles—that grow off each other. They don't have to be complicated to be effective.*

Vest (Left) by Janet Karpack. This woolen vest is another good example of a central shape that grows outward. The tapestry stitch straps were added afterward.

Detail of Vest (Right) by Janet Karpack. Notice the cut-out triangles made by chaining across the tops of the light triangles and edging each one with shrimp stitches.

6. Clothing

Saskia Saffron's Coat *by Frank Lincoln Viner. Although the tapestry stitch design is complex, the shape of his daughter's woolen coat is straight and simple.*

Crochet and clothing just seem to go together. You can make afghans and pillows by the dozens, but there's something about wearing what you've made that's really satisfying. Maybe you like it when strangers come up to you at a party and flip out, or maybe you like the knowledge that you don't need Bloomingdale's to look great. It's different for everyone, but there's a basic pride in turning a pile of wool into a sweater that doesn't exist anywhere in the world but on your back. Portable painting? Maybe.

Why is crochet such a good medium for making clothes? First there's the joy of wearing something you've made. Then there's the question of time—crocheting just doesn't take that long. And you can crochet in any direction, so the process of adding on shapes and fitting the shapes into clothes is very flexible. The variety is also incredible. You can make unbelievably sexy dresses that look as if they'd grown on you, or heavy, sculptural, tightly worked coats that would laugh at Alaska. You have complete control from start to finish—not only are you designing the shape, but

also the fabric that makes the shape. Covering the human body is a very sensual pastime, and crochet seems to be a perfect body covering because it grows in stages—you don't have to know what you're making before you start. And you don't have to begin in any particular place. You can start a blouse at the waist, you can start it in the middle, or you can start at the top—it's all up to you. You can begin with a shape, and that shape suggests another shape, and suddenly you know that it would lie just perfectly on your friend's back. And so it goes until you've made a vest that's totally incredible.

This chapter will teach you the basic methods of constructing things to wear and also how to make them fit you (or someone else) without using patterns. Printed crochet patterns are designed to fit millions of people, but chances are you're not included in the "average" they're supposed to fit. But you can't go wrong when you use a body and fit the garment to it.

The shape of most crocheted clothing is usually simple so the pattern or design can be the focal point. Even when you get into

Vest by Del Feldman. Here's a good example of a simply shaped woolen vest done in separate pieces, buttoned down the sides, and joined at the shoulders. It's lined in jersey.

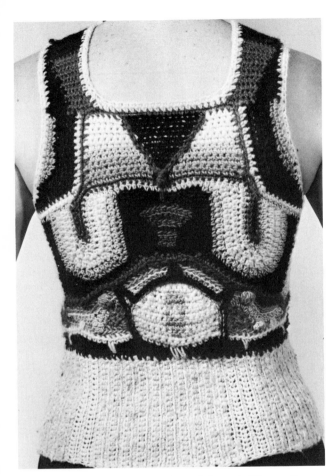

Vest (back) by Arlene Stimmel. The welt was done separately in the rib stitch, with the design worked off it from the bottom up. It's one of the simplest shapes for a top. Vest lent by Jennifer Manne.

more elaborate surface designs, it's a good idea to keep the basic shape as simple as possible. If you're going to wear something, good fit should be your first consideration, so start with simple styles and simple designs until you feel confident.

Crocheting without a Pattern

We've found three ways to avoid the tedious step-by-step crochet patterns for making clothes. The first is to find a paper sewing pattern that will adapt itself to the stretch of crochet. It should be simple, without darts or decoration. The patterns marked "especially for knits" are usually perfect for crochet. After you've got your pattern, crochet the shapes of the pattern pieces, using any stitch or colors that you'd like. If you're using a very stretchy stitch, it's a good idea to measure the paper pieces against your body—you might need one size smaller than you'd usually wear. Keep laying your crocheting on the pattern, but make sure you *eliminate* the ⅝" seam allowance that's given for fabric. When you have all your pieces crocheted, join them with any of the three joining methods given in Chapter 4. After the pieces are joined, edge around the neck, armholes, or sleeves to give it a finished look.

The second way to construct a garment is similar, only instead of using a paper pat-

tern, use some piece of clothing that fits you well but has outlived its usefulness. Take it apart and crochet the pieces in the same way as explained above.

The third method is the most fun and allows you the most freedom. Just hold the work up to you and fit it as you go along. When you have to fit the back or a sleeve, it helps to have someone give you a hand, but you'll be amazed how easy it really is. And if you're making something for someone else, you can custom fit it to them as you go along. If you plan on making a lot of clothing, it pays to get a dressmakers' dummy that you can pin into. It's also a good idea to become familiar with the basic shapes for sleeves, necklines, dresses, tops, pants, and skirts.

Considerations Before You Start

Before you begin to make anything to wear, you've got to consider several things. Is it going to be something that you'll wear a lot, or just on special occasions? Should it be sturdy or delicate? You wouldn't use a very heavy yarn to make a long skirt because the weight would make it stretch all

Sleeve Detail of Vest by Dina Schwartz. This unusually shaped sleeve is draped from the shoulder and not connected anywhere else. It was worked in mohair, wool, and metallics.

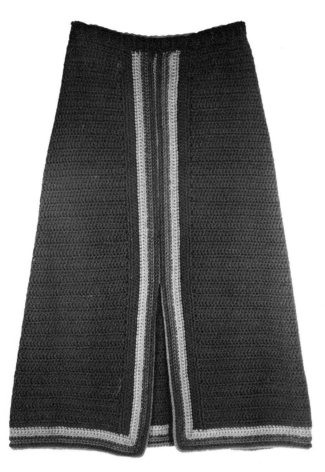

Skirt *by Nicki Hitz Edson. This woolen skirt is simply an open tube joined by a band of stripes down the front. Note the elastic waist, which gets covered by an overblouse.*

out of shape. Lacy openwork stitches have a lot more stretch than tight stitches. You might want to use the stretch of a yarn to your advantage—a shawl made of rayon ribbon would hang beautifully, but a dress made of it would be too heavy to hang well.

It's always a good idea, no matter what yarn you're using, to experiment with it before you start a big project. Make a swatch, pull on it, wet it, give it a real workover and find out its properties. The yarn chart in Chapter 1 will give you a general idea what different yarns are good for, but it's by no means the last word, and who knows what you might find if you experiment. Some basic concepts for clothes and how you would go about crocheting them are shown at the end of this chapter.

After you feel pretty confident about making clothes that fit, you can get into more elaborate things. Ideas can come from many sources—encyclopedias of clothing styles are full of great designs. Flowing medieval sleeves, tunics, Egyptian hangings, Victorian high-necked blouses, and flapper dresses can all be adapted to crochet.

Blocking

Almost anything you crochet will benefit from a good blocking. Basically, this means pressing your pieces so they have a finished look. If you're making something out of several pieces, block each piece before you join them together. If the garment is one piece, block it on one side and then on the other.

If what you've made is definitely washable (and most of the things will be) wash it out in mild soap and then roll it in a thick towel to absorb the excess moisture. Get a dry towel and lay it out flat, then lay the wet garment on it. Don't put it near the heat and don't put it right in the sun. Just let it dry naturally, changing towels to help it dry faster. This is the simplest way to block something, but most things look even better if they're blocked with an iron in the manner described further on in this chapter.

If you'll be making a lot of things, it's a good idea to make a blocking board. A blocking board is a clean, flat surface that you can stick pins into. It should be big enough to hold anything that you're liable to make. Get a piece of plywood (3 feet by 4 feet is a good size) and cover it with a thickness of quilted material, old towels, or anything soft, stapled tightly to the underside of the plywood. Then cover the whole thing with white muslin or lightweight canvas, pulled as tight as possible and stapled to the plywood. Lay the board on sawhorses, or if you don't have room to keep it out all the time, lean it against a wall or store it in the closet.

Detail of Jacket (Above) by Arlene Stimmel. Notice how the large dark shape follows the shape of the body and how the triangles cinch in the waist of this cotton jacket.

Sleeve of Jacket (Right) by Arlene Stimmel. By keeping the body of the jacket simple, the sleeve, which was done in one piece and set in, becomes the focal point.

So, you want to block something. Lay the pieces (or the finished garment) down with the wrong side facing you. Get some rust-proof T-pins (most notions stores have them) and pin the pieces to the board. Pin at a *slant* to the edge of the piece, because if you pin perpendicularly, you'll wind up with a lot of little scallops along the edge. After the pieces are securely pinned, wet a thin dishtowel or cloth, wring it out and lay it on the piece. Press down lightly with a hot iron, steaming each part of the piece. Keep wetting the towel to keep a good steam action going. Make sure you don't run the iron along, just press and lift. And don't block popcorns or other three-dimensional stitches—it will flatten them out and you'll lose the whole effect. Some of the things you make might have to be dry-cleaned, but even if this is the case, they can still be blocked this way.

After the entire piece is steamed, leave it securely in place until it's completely dry. Then remove the pins and you're done.

Besides making a piece look finished, blocking can cover up some mistakes. If a sleeve isn't quite long enough you can stretch it out when you block. The same with an armhole or a leg. But you can't expect to remedy a really bad fit—you'll have to redo that.

Skirts

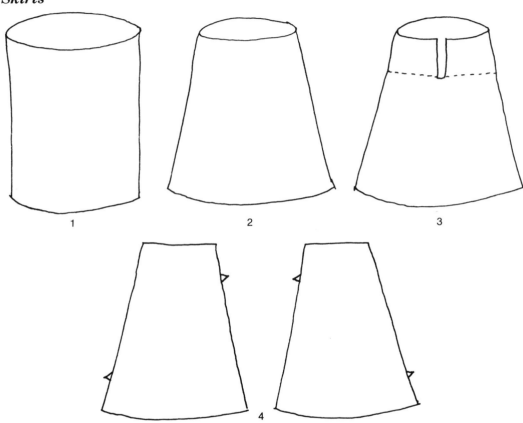

1

2

3

4

1. Think of a skirt as a tube.

2. A skirt worked in the round in one piece. Make sure the opening fits over the hips, and then tighten it with elastic or a drawstring when you're done.

3. A skirt with a tight-fitting waist. Use buttons or a zipper to close the opening.

4. A skirt done in 2 pieces from a paper pattern. Tie pieces of yarn where the tabs fall so you can match the pieces together.

Sleeveless Sweaters and Vests

1. Diagram of a basic sleeveless sweater.

A-A = Back length with welt.
B-B = Half waistline (about 1″ to 2″ smaller
*   than bust width D-D).*
B-C = Height of welt.
C-D = Side length without welt.
D-D = Half bust width below armhole.
E-E = Back width.
F-F = ⅓ of back width for neck.
F-G = Shoulder width, slanted slightly.
D-G = Height of armhole (same as height of
*   sleeve head if you add sleeves).*
A-H = Depth of neck, about 2″ to 3″.

*2. A sweater is also basically a tube. It can be
started with a chain measured at the bust below the armhole and worked down. Or it can be
started with a chain measured at the waist or
hips and worked upward.*

*3. After you've completed the body, join the
yarn about 1½″ in from the edge on the front
and work in rows until you reach the neckline.
Decrease accordingly and work each strap separately. Do the same on the back and then
make a seam at the shoulders.*

*4. If you want a welt it can be either crocheted
or knitted. If crocheted, make a strip as wide as
you want it (rib stitch is good for this), join it
into a band, and crochet the body off it. If knitted, add it onto the finished body by picking up
the stitches of the body on circular needles.*

*5. For a vest, just leave a front opening. Work
in rows, keeping the front opening vertical on
each side. Then add the straps the same as for a
pullover.*

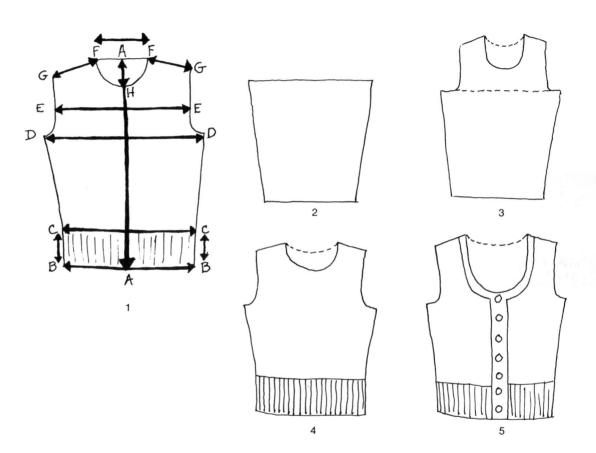

Dresses

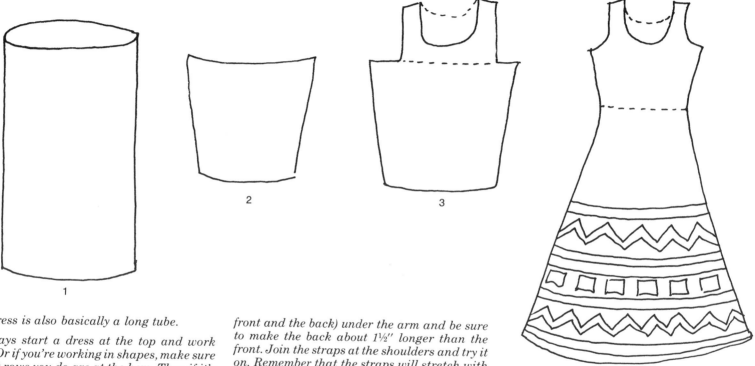

1. *A dress is also basically a long tube.*

2. *Always start a dress at the top and work down. Or if you're working in shapes, make sure the last rows you do are at the hem. Then if it's too long (or stretches out) you can shorten it. Start with a chain around the bust, right below the armholes. Work down to the waist in the round, decreasing slightly. Mark the exact sides with pieces of yarn so you can keep the decreases right on top of each other.*

3. *Then add the straps on the front and the back. Be sure to leave at least 3" (1½" on the*

front and the back) under the arm and be sure to make the back about 1½" longer than the front. Join the straps at the shoulders and try it on. Remember that the straps will stretch with the weight of the skirt so don't make them too long. Also be sure the waist isn't so tight that you can't slip the dress on over your head.

4. *When the top fits, join the yarn at the waist and continue in the round for the skirt, increasing for a flared effect. Then you can add on sleeves, a collar, a belt, or any other trim.*

Sleeves

1. *This sleeve is added right onto the armhole. Join the yarn at the underarm and edge around the armhole. Work in rounds, decreasing under the arm so the sleeve won't bunch. Then make the sleeve as long as you want. Keep track of what you do on one sleeve so the other will be identical. You might have to increase slightly on the top of the sleeve. For a flared effect, increase more on the top but keep the underarm decrease the same.*

2. *For a puffed sleeve, increase generously on the top and side. Then decrease all around to get a tight cuff.*

3. *A sweater with a set-in or fitted sleeve (done as a separate piece and then set in). When you set in a sleeve, turn the body of the sweater inside out, but keep the sleeve right side out. Lay the sleeve inside the body and make a seam around the armhole, matching all the underarm seams. When you turn the body right side out, the sleeve will be attached with the seam on the inside. If you have to gather the sleeve to make it fit, just skip a few stitches—it won't show on the finished seam.*

4. *Diagram of a long set-in sleeve.*

A-A = Outer arm length with welt (measure with your arm stretched out).
B-B = Wrist width.
B-C = Height of welt.
C-D = Inner arm length without welt.
D-D = Upper arm width below armhole.
E-E = Width of sleeve head, about 2″ or 3″.
A-F = Height of sleeve head: outer arm length minus inner arm length with welt (same as height of armhole).
D-B = Seam line joined before sleeve set in.

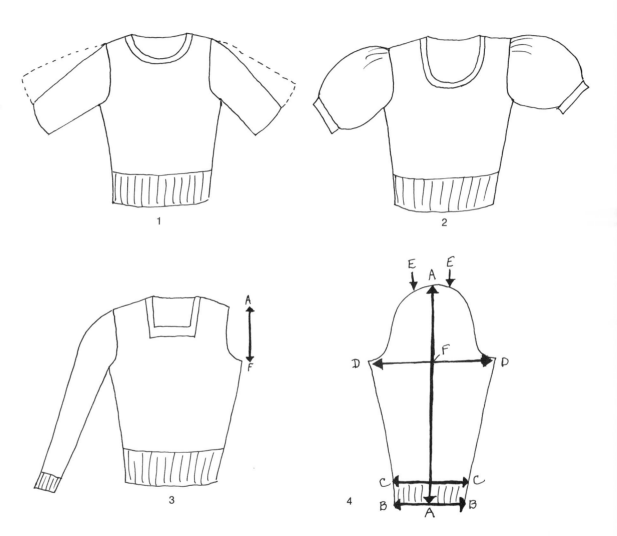

Pants

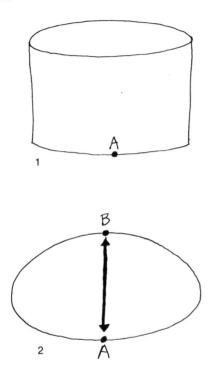

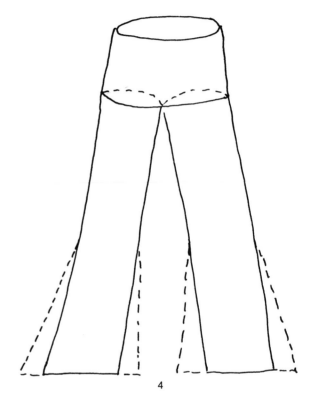

1. Pants are basically 3 tubes. Start with a chain at the waist (or hip) and go down to the crotch.

2. This is a view looking down on the tube you've just made. Mark the middle of the front (A) and the middle of the back (B). Try it on and measure the distance between these two points.

Join the yarn at A, make a chain that long, and attach it at B.

3. Start working in the round for the first leg, picking up the crotch chains. Make the leg as long as you want.

4. Make another chain the same length as the first one from A to B. Do the second leg the same as the first, picking up the crotch chains. Join the crotch seam on the inside and you have a pair of pants. If you want bell-bottoms, increase gradually on both sides of the legs. The waist can either be elastic or have an opening. If you want hip-huggers, start your first tube at the hips and tighten it later with a drawstring.

Hats

Basically, a hat is very simple. Think of it as a circle with a tube attached. Begin by making a circle big enough to fit the top of your head. Then increase only enough so that the shape fits your head snugly. A simply shaped hat can look elaborate if you use lots of colors and stitches. Or you can add lots of relief stitches after the shape is right. Earflaps, a brim, or a cuff can also be added. Helmets, stocking caps, and berets are other hat shapes you might try. The helmet shown in the photo on the left is by Arlene Stimmel. The cowboy hat on the right is by Mark Dittrick. To make the tight stitches he says you have to put band-aids on your fingers and masking tape on your hook to avoid blisters. We believe him.

Bags

Any shape that can hold things can be made into a bag: a tube makes a long skinny one; a long rectangle can be folded into an envelope and seamed up the sides; a large circle can be tightened on the top with a drawstring. These are just a few of the many shapes you can try. If you use an open stitch, the bag can be lined with leather or heavy material. Just cut the pieces to correspond to the crocheted pieces, seam them, and sew them in place. Then the lining color will show through the stitches for a three-dimensional effect. If you're making a shoulder bag, be sure to make the strap a little shorter than you think you'll need, because the strap will stretch with weight inside. The pouch bag above is by Susan Morrow. The rose bag on the right is by Janet Lipkin Decker.

Mittens

There are two ways to make mittens. The first is to trace the outline of your hand on a piece of paper and crochet two pieces to fit the tracing. Then seam them together and add a cuff. The second way is to start the shape at the tips of your fingers and work in the round. Keep trying it on and leave a hole where the thumb will go. Then continue working until you reach the wrist. To make the thumb, add on a tube that decreases to a point. Or, if you'd like, you can start at the wrist and work to the fingertips. It's all up to you. The mittens shown were made by Arlene Stimmel and lent by Marty Schlass.

Boots by Nicki Hitz Edson. You wouldn't want to wear these in a snowstorm, but they'll sure keep your feet warm around the house. They're basically a tube with feet added and leather crocheted to the bottom.

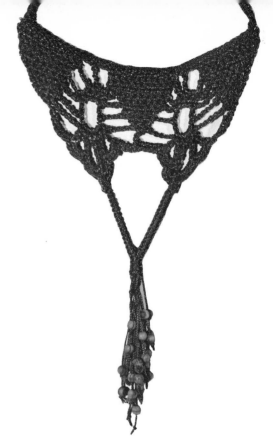

Necklace *(Above) by Joan Wortis. A very delicate hanging worked in rayon in single crochet and chains.*

Necklace *(Left) by Norma Minkowitz. This wall hanging for your body was made in cotton string and shows a good way to experiment with shapes and stitches.*

Bobo's Coat *(Right) by Pat Mueller. This is the last word in clothing. What can we say?*

7. Color, Design, and Ideas

Starry Vest by Dina Schwartz. Dina generally works her designs from drawings, so she has definite control over the placement of her images. It was worked in wool, mohair, metallics, and synthetics, and the outline of the swan was embroidered to make it stand out.

Color is a difficult thing to talk about. Even if you've had training, it tends to be very subjective. We're not going to get into the technical aspects of vocabulary and the color wheel, but if you're interested in color theory, there are many good books on the subject. We prefer to stress color practice; how should you think of color in relationship to crochet?

The best approach is to develop a color awareness—using yarns that work well together to give a desired effect. And a lot of this is personal taste. Your best textbooks are the yarn charts distributed by the yarn companies. How many times have you thumbed through a cookbook, thinking: "maybe I'll try that recipe sometime." Approach these charts with the same spirit. Learn how colors work next to each other, try combinations that are unusual, be conscious of color groups (different shades of purple and blue, for example), and be aware of the many beautiful, natural colors that aren't dyed at all. Some crocheters just aren't happy with the yarn colors available so they get into dyeing their own. But this is a whole other subject.

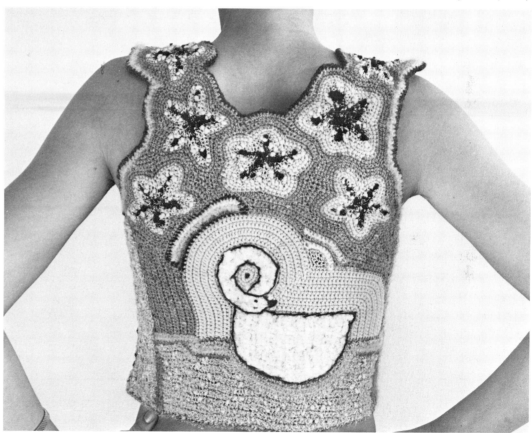

Be aware of the colors you see around you every day. You'll be amazed how many ideas you can get looking at what people wear, at a vegetable stand, at an autumn field, or at the plants in your apartment.

When you get into choosing designs for your projects, there are unlimited possibilities. As you thumb through this book, notice all the different styles in different peoples' work. How did they decide on their designs, and where did their ideas come from?

First of all, you have the choice of working figuratively or abstractly. Figurative work uses images that can be recognized for what they are—a tree or a swan. Abstract work takes images and reduces them to their basic shapes so they're not literal but rather suggest where they came from. Then you can work with geometric shapes, hard-edge triangles, squares, etc., that are separate from one another. Or you can use expressionistic shapes, where the forms and colors flow into each other in a freer way. Designs can be symmetrical: draw an imaginary line down the middle and both sides are the same. Or they can be asymmetrical,

with both sides different. These are the basic elements of design, but within each category, there are endless possibilities. Some styles just fit some peoples' working methods and tastes. With practice, you'll find which suits yours.

Sources for design are everywhere. One of the best is the good old museum, with its historical examples of crafts—oriental rugs, folk art, tapestries, African masks, Navajo rugs, or early American quilts. Not only are these designs readily adapted to crochet, but the colors are fantastic. Take a sketch book with you when you go to museums and be on the look out for ideas. It's not that you want to copy anything—it's more to see how other cultures expressed themselves and get ideas for things you might want to crochet. If you're not near museums, books will give you the same treat.

Another source of ideas is simply what interests you. The everyday things that you tend to take for granted can be a good source of inspiration. The food in your kitchen, the seasons, nature, or your pet dog. Or fantasies of places you'd like to go, mythical animals, dreams, or tarot cards. Just use your imagination.

Some people like to plan out a design before they begin to crochet. Others just start somewhere and let the design grow by itself. As you work more you'll discover your own methods. Most of the work in this book wasn't planned first, it just happened.

As we mentioned in the materials chapter, a specific type of yarn can inspire a project. If you're doing a Mexican-inspired pillow, what better yarn to use than Mexican handspun? The texture of a certain yarn might lend itself to a three-dimensional design, and brilliant-colored yarn would lend itself to hard-edged geometric shapes. There's no way to cover all the sources for ideas—your eyes are your most important tool. Keep them sharp and in good working order.

Detail of Jungle Cape (Left) *by Frank Lincoln Viner. These happy animals were done in the tapestry stitch with wool yarn. The thickness of the rows is caused by the yarn carried along and it makes a texture of its own.*

Wall Hanging (Right) *by Cindy Picchi. Symmetrical designs often tend to become faces, and this hanging, made of wool yarn, becomes another face when turned upside down.*

Detail of Vest (Left) by Sharron Hedges. Using basic geometric shapes and wool yarn, Sharron made this **almost** symmetrical design. Notice how the triangles at the top and the hook shapes at the bottom are the same shapes but worked in different colors.

Vest (Right) by Diana Schmidt. This a good example of a totally asymmetrical design.

George's Vest (Far Right) by Del Feldman. The symmetrical candle shapes on each side give this vest a baroque quality. The ornate pockets are classic afghan squares. The vest was worked in wool and has leather buttons.

Malcolm's Vest *(Above) by Del Feldman. The simplification of figurative shapes gives this vest a primitive quality. (Lent by Malcolm Varon).*

Detail of Malcolm's Vest *(Right). The popcorns and picots add a three-dimensional quality to this otherwise flat design.*

Dolman Sweater by Dina Schwartz. A combination of mohair, wool, cotton, metallic, and synthetic yarns add to the fantasy effect. Dina drew the asymmetrical design first, then worked the vest mostly in the tapestry stitch.

Backless Choli by Arlene Stimmel. Worked in rayon ribbon and linen, this top really molds to the body. All that keeps it on are a strap across the back and two strings that tie around the neck. Notice the openwork scallops at the bottom. Vest lent by Judy Ley.

Blue Landscape by Arlene Stimmel. This design, worked in cotton and rayon, was conceived as a wearable painting. Notice the knitted welt, which was added last for a better fit. Vest lent by Deanna Levy.

Clam Vest by Dina Schwartz. This is a good example of Dina's mixed yarns and tapestry stitch designs.

Jamaican Landscape (Right) by Arlene Stimmel. This vest was inspired by an antique quilted pillow and by the lush colors of Jamaica. It's made of rayon ribbon and cotton and worked mostly in single crochet. Vest lent by Dione Hemberger.

Fish Bag *(Above) by Nicki Hitz Edson. The multi-colored scales are individual shell stitches worked off a base of double crochet.*

Wool Boots *(Left) by Nicki Hitz Edson. The simple, graphic design owes much of its richness to the warm, Persian-inspired colors. The soles are leather.*

Tartar Helmet *(Right) by Nicki Hitz Edson. The rich colors of the Swedish wool are reminiscent of Persian carpets. The rose-colored shape on the side is knitted.*

Wool Hanging *(Far Right) by Cindi Picchi. This piece, about 3½ feet long, incorporates feathers and beads, which add to its primitive feeling.*

Bird Coat by Janet Lipkin Decker. Would you believe this is crocheted? The rich use of three-dimensional stitches and shapes makes this a wearable sculpture. Coat lent by Susan Zises.

Detail of Sleeve. There's a surprise under each layer of this incredible coat. The green design under her hand is a blow-up of a small design on the back.

Detail of Back. The subtle mixing of colors is a result of vegetable dyeing and good color sense. The off-white background yarn is handspun wool from Equador.

Cloud Coat by Sharron Hedges. This is an incredible example of mixing simple color areas with elaborate details. Most of the wool is vegetable dyed and the clouds are brushed mohair. Coat lent by Marlo Sloan.

Detail of Back. Because of the sparse use of metallic yarn, the sunburst takes on three-dimensional depth.

Detail of Sleeve. The three-dimensional shape under the shoulder makes the cap puff out.

Medieval Blouse by Sharron Hedges. This wool blouse is lined in jersey so it can be worn next to the body. The elaborate top sleeves are layered over the simpler blue sleeves.

Detail of Front.

Detail of Back.

Afghan by Jackie Henderson. 3 feet by 4 feet and worked in wool knitting worsted, this simple design is reminiscent of an oriental rug.

Great Coat *(front).*

Great Coat *(back) by Frank Lincoln Viner. Influenced by both Kabuki robes and a trip to Turkey, Frank's magnificent woolen tapestry stitch coat weighs about 40 pounds.*

Ronald's Hat by Nicki Hitz Edson. Nicki really captured the feeling of the hat in Ron's self-portrait. It was crocheted in Irish wool yarn.

Self-portrait by Ronald Edson. Ron painted this self-portrait in an imaginery hat, which gave Nicki the idea to crochet it.

Yosha Bear—Nicki's dog.

Wolf Mask by Nicki Hitz Edson. *This woolen mask was obviously inspired by Yosha, who really is part wolf.*

Beaded Bib by Lannie Martowe. The metallic beads, the openwork stitches, and the flower give this woolen bib a Victorian look. Lannie worked the design from a drawing.

Indonesian-inspired Hat by Ann Stearnbach. An experiment with many types of stitches in wool yarn turned into a stuffed hat.

8. Sculpture

Horn-nosed Hand Puppet by Mark Dittrick. Mark found a bicycle horn and it had to be a nose for a puppet. The Harpo wig was made by doing a square of very tight single crochet, ironing the hell out of it, and then unraveling it. Then it's cut into lengths and hooked onto the head.

Detail of Wolf Mask by Nicki Hitz Edson. The snout and jaw are stuffed, the tongue just worked in the round (the complete mask is shown in Chapter 7).

Now that you've worked in flat shapes, the basic concepts of crochet are under your belt. This chapter deals with expanding this knowledge into the construction of three-dimensional forms. By rounding out and adding onto a two-dimensional shape, it can become a mask, a stuffed animal, a plant-holder, or an abstract landscape. You just have to take your thinking one step further into the round. These forms are a little tricky to construct, so we've listed a number of ways to approach them.

The first method is to use a stiff yarn and let it mold itself into the shape. Mark Dittrick's horn-nosed hand puppet was done this way—he used a very tight single crochet. When you put your hand into it, it comes alive, but it will stand on its own even without a hand.

The second method is to use a pattern, as we explained in the clothing chapter. But instead of using a paper sewing pattern, you have to make your own pattern out of paper, muslin, or cheap cotton. Cut out the pieces you'll need, keep fitting them together, and when you've got it right, take them apart. Then crochet each piece following the pattern and join them together. This method is good for a shape made of a lot of simple shapes (like a geometric solid) or for a complex shape that you want to visualize before you begin to crochet.

The third method is to crochet flat pieces without patterns and join them together to make a three-dimensional shape. For instance, the snout on Nicki's wolf mask was done in two pieces. The top part was made larger and was shaped so it would fit well over the top of the mouth. They were crocheted together, stuffed, and then the picot teeth were added.

The fourth method is good for large pieces. Make an armature out of chicken wire, bending and cutting it until it reaches the desired form. Then cover it with Dacron stuffing and muslin. If you want it to be extra strong, you can stuff the chicken wire also. After you've got the shape right, crochet over it. Cindy made the body of her swan this way. A heavy wire covered with stuffing forms the base for the neck, which can bend in any direction.

The last method is to create, sew, and stuff a muslin form like a large doll. Then you have the whole form to follow as you cover it with crochet. This method is good because the stuffing won't ever come through the crochet. Pat's bird dragon was done this way.

Again, we're going to demonstrate the basic techniques with a sampler. The basic shape in the sampler is a tube that expands and contracts, and has other tubes coming off it. The directions for it are very general, because we just want to start you off experimenting with sculptural shapes and relief stitches. Don't worry about the lack of specific directions—instead, follow the basic concepts and come up with your own sculptured shapes.

Basic Sampler Shape

Step 1. *Begin by making a tube. It's simply a ring of chains worked off in the round, without increasing or decreasing.*

Step 2. *After you've got a few inches of straight tube, turn it into a bulb. This is done by increasing like you did in the circle, making sure the work doesn't ruffle or buckle.*

Step 3. *When the middle of the bulb is as big as you want it, stop increasing for several rounds.*

Step 4. *Then begin to decrease at approximately the same rate as you increased.*

Step 5. *When the tube is back to the original size, work several rounds straight.*

Step 6. *On this section of the tube, you want to leave holes for the branches. Where you want one, chain 5 or so, skip the same number of stitches, and continue with the round. Then pick the chain stitches up again on the next round. (This is also the way you make buttonholes.) Make 3 holes in 3 different places along the tube.*

Step 7. *To make the minaret for the top, start a bulb as before and then decrease slowly until it comes to a point.*

Details of Sampler

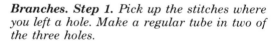

Branches. Step 1. *Pick up the stitches where you left a hole. Make a regular tube in two of the three holes.*

Step 2. *In the third hole, make a bent tube. Think of an elbow—there must be more rows on the outside of the bend than on the inside. Choose which way you want the tube to bend, then work back and forth around the outside of the bend, joining each row with a slip stitch or two. When you have enough of a curve, continue with the tube as before.*

Relief Stitches and "Springs." Step 1. *Relief stitches can be picked up off any existing base of stitches and you can work them in any direction you like. Begin by doing a round of single crochet a few rows up from the bottom of the main shape. To make a stitch, insert the hook around the stitch you're working off.*

Step 2. *Join on another color and start going up the shape, picking up each stitch with double crochet. Practice snaking the stitches, going in different directions. This will give you a high, raised line.*

Step 3. *Start again down by the first row of relief singles. Join on another color and start snaking, but do 4 doubles in each stitch, this time for a ruffled effect.*

Step 4. *To make the hanging "springs" off the bent branch, make a chain as long as you want the spring to be. Work back on the chain, picking up only the top part of each chain stitch and do 2 singles in each one. This will automatically give you a curlicue effect. If they don't curl enough, try doing 3 singles in each chain.*

Flowers. Step 1. *To make a very ruffled flower on one of the straight branches, pick up the stitches on the end of the branch and increase a lot (2 or 3 stitches in each stitch). Keep increasing in each round.*

Step 2. *Make another ruffled flower on the other straight branch. (This one is in the back, you can't see it on the picture.)*

Step 3. *Another type of flower can be made by picking up the third from last row of the bent branch with a round of relief single crochet (A). Make fingers off this round, using 2 different colors. Then pick up the second from the last row with single and make a finger in every stitch (B). Pick up the last row of the branch with single, work even for about 1", and increase a lot to give a daffodil effect (C). Add more onto it if you want to and then stuff the whole shape.*

Swan by Cindy Picchi. Stuffed animals tend to be cute, but the delicate handling of the head gives this swan the elegance of the real thing.

Bird Dragon by Pat Mueller. Every stitch and shape Pat could think of is put together in this flaming creature, which stands about 2 feet high and is made of wool rug yarn.

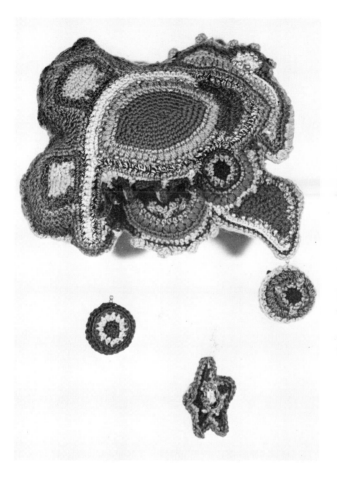

Abstract Hanging by Suzannah Lewis. This is a good example of using a variety of yarns to produce a rich, three-dimensional texture. The whole shape, which is 4 feet long, serves as a bag for the macramé monkey fists.

Climbing Fox by Pat Mueller. This sure beats taxidermy. Notice the stuffed mushrooms below the tree. It's about 1 foot high.

Stuffed Mobile by Susan Morrow. Basically an unusually shaped pillow with dangles. Susan hangs this piece from her ceiling.

Frog (Above) by Nicki Hitz Edson. It's worked in rug yarn.

Woman on Appliqué Pillow (Right) by Norma Minkowitz. The crocheted cotton figure is in bas-relief on a woven, crocheted, and appliquéd pillow. About 6" high.

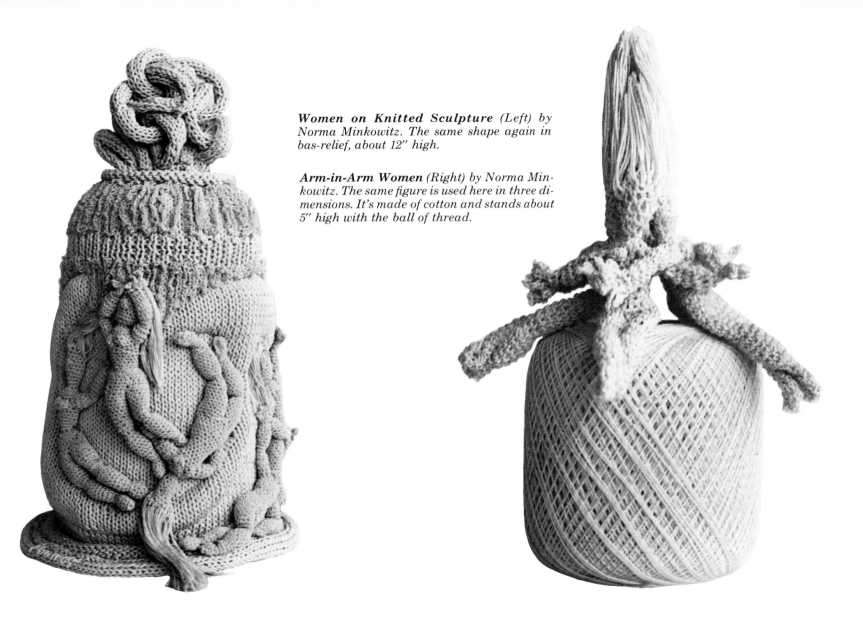

Women on Knitted Sculpture *(Left) by Norma Minkowitz. The same shape again in bas-relief, about 12″ high.*

Arm-in-Arm Women *(Right) by Norma Minkowitz. The same figure is used here in three dimensions. It's made of cotton and stands about 5″ high with the ball of thread.*

Caterpillar by Diana Schmidt. Another flaming creature, about 1 foot high.

Kris Kringle by Lannie Martowe. This realistic interpretation, worked in wool and cotton, resembles an antique doll and is about 1½ feet high.

Satyr Mask by Nicki Hitz Edson.

Bird Mask by Nicki Hitz Edson.

Mystery Mask by Nicki Hitz Edson. Nicki's masks, like primitive ones, can be worn either to ward off evil spirits or can stand by themselves. They're all worked in wool.

9. Junk and Mixed Media

Section of African Voodoo Man by Lannie Martowe. The shells in this wool headdress are crocheted in, the feathers and leather sewed in, and the horseshoe crab tails tied in. Notice the embroidered eyes.

Beaded Muff by Lannie Martowe. This was an old fur muff that Lannie's dog chewed up. Instead of throwing it out she took off the fur, crocheted the cover, and strung glass beads from the bottom. Then she lined it in pink satin.

There's no rule that says crochet has to be done only with yarn. All kinds of junk can be incorporated as part of a design—beads, rings, stones, shells, bells, buttons, and found objects—either as decorative extras or practical additions. If you're a scavenger (and who isn't these days) your best finds can find their way into your crochet. Crochet can also be combined with numerous other crafts—leathercraft, macramé, ceramics, metalwork, weaving, knitting, needlepoint, appliqué, and sewing. So if you're already involved in one of these crafts, crochet offers an opportunity to take them a step further.

Beads

Because beads are so beautiful and can define shapes so well, they're especially suited to crochet designs. The easiest way to use them is to string them on your working yarn before you're ready to add it to the design. Get some microcrystalline sculptors' wax from an art supply store: no other wax seems to work because they all crumble instead of sticking to the yarn. Soften it in your fingers and run the end of the yarn over it until the point is stiff enough to thread through the beads. Make sure the hole in the bead is big enough to handle the yarn. String more beads than you think you'll need because, once you start to work, you can't add more beads without starting a new piece of yarn. The beads are crocheted right into the work—as you want one, slide it down close to the hook and do a regular single crochet, yarning over with the yarn on the left side of the bead. Beads should always be worked in with the wrong side of the work facing you, then they'll show up on the right side. You can add a bead for every stitch or skip a few; it depends on the effect you want. Just slide a bead down and crochet around it as before. This method also works with shells, buttons, or anything else with a hole in it that can be strung onto the yarn.

If you want to incorporate stuff with large holes such as rings, bells or buckles, just catch them where you want them with one or more stitches of single crochet. Insert your hook into the stitch and catch the object as you yarn over. Think of it as crocheting a stick into a row—each stitch goes around it.

If you want to add something that has no hole, like a stone, crochet a holder for it, decreasing to fit the shape as you hold it in place with your left hand. Make sure the last row is tight enough so it won't fall out. Then catch the base of the holder with new yarn and crochet it firmly into the body of your work.

Crochet and Other Materials

Combining crochet with other crafts and materials is growing more and more popular. This combination is practical as well as esthetic—maybe you want an area of fabric in a design that has no stretch at all, or maybe you want to incorporate an antique piece of needlepoint into a vest. Once again, there are endless possibilities.

One of the most practical combinations is leather and crochet. The smooth richness of leather works so well with the texture of yarn. And if you're the lazy type, it takes much less time to work off a piece of leather than to crochet a piece the same size. But

Necklace with Coral and Shells *(Left) by Peri Trout. The coral was glued in place and the shells caught with yarn and then glued.*

Detail of a Long Dress *(Right) by Arlene Stimmel. The center of the star is suede edged in the blanket stitch. The gold beads were crocheted in as she went along. Dress lent by Paula Barr.*

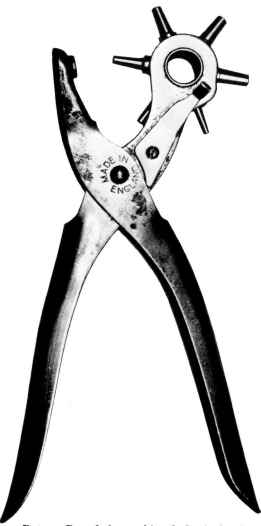

Rotary Punch *for making holes in leather.*

this technique poses special problems and you should plan pretty carefully since the price of leather is nothing to sneer at.

First of all you must fit the materials to what you want to make. Leather can be used for just about anything—vests, pillows, bags, dresses, etc. If you're going to make something for a body make sure you pick a leather that's soft and fluid. If you want a bag or a belt you need a good strong skin that won't stretch out. After you pick the leather, the next step is choosing the crochet material. It should be compatible with the type of leather you've decided on—you wouldn't want a heavy rug yarn with a delicate deerskin. String (linen or cotton) seems to be better than yarn for articles that get a lot of wear because it doesn't stretch out as much.

Okay, you've got your leather and your yarn and you've decided what you're going to make. First you have to edge the leather with yarn so that you can crochet off it. There are several ways to do this, and they all involve punching holes. A rotary punch with an adjustable wheel containing six punches of different sizes is the best tool for this. Working from the wrong side of the leather, draw a line ¼″ to ½″ in from the edge. Take a piece of scrap and try the hole size you think would best hold the yarn you plan to use. If the yarn fits easily through the hole then the size is right. Space the

holes by eye . . . closer together for a fine yarn and further apart for a heavy one. Punch holes all around the piece, spacing them as evenly as possible.

The next step is to add the yarn to the leather so you have a base to crochet off of. There are three ways to do this, each giving a different effect.

The first is to thread a length of yarn through a yarn needle and do an embroidery blanket stitch around the leather. Keep the tension even so the leather doesn't buckle. Then crochet around the piece, catching each loop as if it were a stitch. If you do this in a contrasting color yarn you'll get little lines all along the leather so your holes must really be even. If you do it in the same color as the leather it won't show as much.

The second method gives a definite hard-edged look. Using a smaller hook than you'll be crocheting with, insert it right into each hole and make a succession of chain stitches. The reason for using the smaller hook is so you don't stretch out the hole with the large one (it would take a huge hole to accommodate a G hook). Don't pull the stitches too tight! Go around the leather, adding an extra chain if you have to keep the corners flat. Then pick up the back part of each chain with the yarn and the regular size hook. Crochet your design right off the chain stitch base.

The third method is to insert the smaller hook right into the holes and single crochet off the leather. This gives you an effect similar to the blanket stitch. But because you have two thicknesses of yarn in each hole the hole must be bigger, and consequently, the leather weaker. We don't recommend this method but many people seem to like it. Try all three and decide for yourself. The most important thing to remember is that the yarn shouldn't pull on the leather—it should have just enough tension to be secure without buckling.

The methods described for leather are the same for other materials, only you don't have to punch holes first. With fabric, weaving, and needlepoint, it's necessary to turn under a hem on the wrong side so the material won't unravel and is thick and strong where the join is. With knitting and macramé you can usually insert the yarn needle or crochet hook right into the holes made by these techniques.

If you do your own metalwork or ceramics, try some pieces with holes in them for yarn. The blanket stitch method would work best on non-flexible materials, and use a good strong yarn or cord that won't break from abrasion. Or try some jewelry with gold or silver and delicate yarn. You'll probably be able to think up many more ideas, but we hope this basic information will get you going.

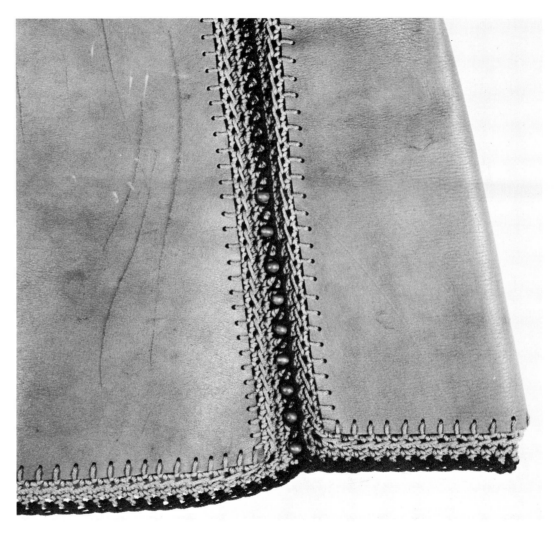

Blanket Stitch *worked off leather.*

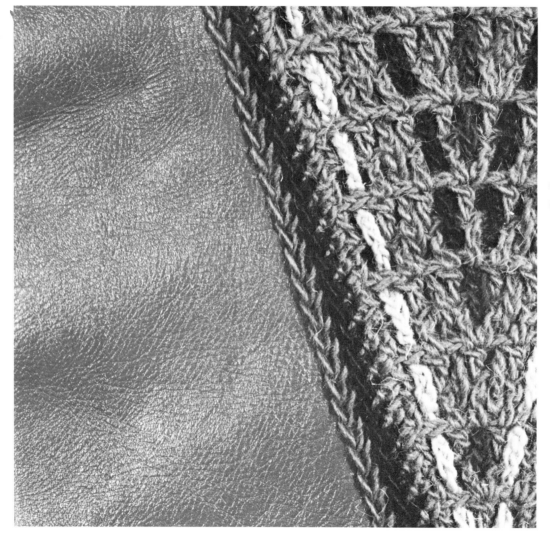

Single Crochet (Above) worked off leather.

Slip Stitch (Left) worked off leather.

Collar (Right) by Debbie Einbender. The filet crochet done in rayon cord and the leather work well together to make this stiff but not unwieldy collar. The leather is pieced and joined with embroidery stitches.

Knitted Ornament (Left) by Norma Minkowitz. This cotton piece is mainly knitted, but has crocheted relief stitches and edges.

Man's Vest (Right) by Suzannah Lewis. She found the telephone I.D. tags in a junk shop and incorporated them into this unusual woolen vest.

Suppliers List

Yarns

J. Hyslop Bathgate & Co.
Galashiels, Scotland
Good variety of suiting,
tapestry, and blanket wools.

Berga/Ullman
P.O. Box 831
1 Westerly Rd.
Ossining, New York 10562
Swedish wools. Samples, $3.00

C. L. Blomquist
A. F. Fritsla, Sweden
Swedish yarns.

B & M Yarn Company
151 Essex Street
New York, New York 10002
Wools, mohair, synthetics.

Briggs & Little Woolen Mill
York Mills
Harvey Station P.O.
York County, N.B., Canada
Wool.

William Condon & Sons
65 Queen Street
Charlottetown, P.E.I., Canada
Wool.

Conlin Yarns
P.O. Box 11812
Philadelphia, Pennsylvania 19128
Wool, tweeds.

Contessa Yarns
P.O. Box 37
Lebanon, Connecticut 06249
Novelty yarns, silk, wools.

Cooper Kenworthy Inc.
564 Eddy Street
P.O. Box 6032
Providence, Rhode Island
Rug wools, novelties, mohair,
cashmere.

Coulter Studios
138 East 60th St.
New York, New York 10022
Swedish rug yarns.

Countryside Handweavers
P.O. Box 1743
Estes Park, Colorado 80517
Imported rug wools, linen, cowhair.
Samples 50c

Craftsman's Mark Ltd.
36 Shoreheath Rd.
Farnham, Surrey, England
Natural color wools.
Samples $1.00

Craft Yarns of Rhode Island
P.O. Box 385
Pawtucket, Rhode Island 02862
Wool, linen, silk, synthetics.

CUM
5 Rosemersgrade
1362 Copenhagen K
Denmark
Rug yarns, linen.
Samples $3.00

Curl Bros., Textiles
334 Lauder Avenue
Toronto 10
Ontario, Canada
Rug wools.
Samples $1.00

Dharma Trading Co.
P.O. Box 1288
Berkeley, California 94701
Wools, linen, synthetics.

Frederick J. Fawcett, Inc.
129 South St.
Boston, Massachusetts 02111
Linen.
Samples $1.00

Filature Sutton Yarns
12 Main St.
Sutton, Quebec, Canada
Wool, yarn winder.

Folklorico
P.O. Box 625
Palo Alto, California
Mexican yarns.
Samples 75c

T. T. French
McNab Street
Hamilton, Ontario, Canada
Natural jute and twines.

A. K. Graupner
Corner House, Valley Road
Bradford, England
Mill ends, wool, alpaca, mohair.

John Hall
Irish Tweed Manufacturing Co.
Crumlin, Co. Antrim
Northern Ireland
Wool yarns, tweeds.

William Hall & Co.
177 Stanley Road
Cheadle Hulme
Cheshire, England
Cotton yarns.

Handcraft Wools
Box 378
Streetsville, Ontario, Canada
Yarns and fleece for dyeing.

Harrisville Designs
P.O. Box 51
Harrisville, New Hampshire 03450
Wool.

Home Yarns Co.
1849 Coney Island Ave.
Brooklyn, New York 11230
Novelties. Samples 35c

House of Yarns and Fabrics
Box 98
Hampton, New Hampshire 03842
Wools.

T. M. Hunter
Brora, Scotland
Harris tweed yarns. Samples $1.00

Husfliden
Bergen-Norway
Grunglagt 1895
Wools, linen.

Filature Lemieux Inc.
St. Ephrem, Beauce
Quebec, Canada
Rug wool, fleece.

Lily Mills
Handweaving Department
Shelby, North Carolina 28150
Cotton and linen.
Samples $1.00

F. MacAusland & Sons
Bloomfield
P.E.I., Canada
Wools.

Macramé & Weaving Supply Co.
63 East Adams Street
Chicago, Illinois 60603
Wool, mohair, jute, cotton, linen.

The Mannings
Creative Crafts.
East Berlin, Pennsylvania 17316
Rug wools.

Mexiskeins
c/o Sharon Murfin
P.O. Box 1624
Missoula, Montana 59801
Mexican handspun yarns,
good colors. Samples $1.00

The Multiple Fabric Co.
Dudley Hill
Bradford, 4 England
Horsehair, camelhair, mohair.

Nature's Fibers
109 Tinker St.
Woodstock, New York
Silk.

Needlewoman Shop
146 Regent Street
London, W.1., England
Wools, assorted yarns, hooks,
leaflets, books.

Niddy Noddy
416 Albany Post Road
Croton-on-Hudson, New York
Good variety of wools and linen.

Norsk Kunstveygarn
Huelfildt Lund
Homborsund pr.
Grimstad, Norway
Natural yarns.
Samples $2.00

Pirates Cove
Box 152
Bayport, L.I., New York 11705
Irish oiled yarns.

Robin & Russ Handweavers
533 North Adams Street
McMinnville, Oregon 97128
Silk, synthetics, wool, linen, jute.

School Products
312 E. 23rd St.
New York, New York 10010
CUM yarns.

Seaboard Twine & Cordage
49 Murray St.
New York, New York 10013
Marine twines.

Shuttlecraft, Inc.
P.O. Box 6041
Providence, Rhode Island 02904
Cotton, wool, synthetics.
Samples 50c

Paula Simmons
Suquamish, Washington 98392
Handspun wools.

Small Fortune
420 S. El Camino Real
Tustin, California 92680
Silk, wool, Mexican handspun,
Haitian cotton.

Stanley Woolen Company
140 Mendon Street
Uxbridge, Massachusetts
Assorted yarns and mohair.
Samples $1.00

The String Thing
1210 Wightman St.
Pittsburgh, Pennsylvania 15217
Linen, Swiss wools, jute, chenille.
Samples $1.50

Studio Del
19 E. 7th St.
New York, New York 10003
Variety of wools and synthetics.

Tahki Imports
336 West End Avenue
New York, New York 10023
Greek handspun, Irish yarns.

Texere Yarns
9 Peckover St.
Bradford 1, Yorkshire, England
Wools and novelties.

Frederich Traub
K.G. 705 Waiblingen
Bei Stuttgart, Germany
Rug wools.

Threadbare Unlimited
20 Cornelia Street
New York, New York 10014
Variety of wools and synthetics.

Vargarnalagvet
Bredgatan 10
222 21 Lund, Sweden
Wool, cowhair.

Washington Paper Company
26 Hudson St.
New York, New York
Cotton, jute, utility twines.

Clinton Wilkinson
6429 Virginia Ave.
Charlotte, North Carolina
Novelty wools, mohair.

The Yarn Center
866 Sixth Ave.
New York, New York
Wools, synthetics.

The Yarn Depot, Inc.
545 Sutter Street
San Francisco, California 94102
Rug wools, import, novelty.
Samples $1.00

Yarn Primitives
P.O. Box 1013
Weston, Connecticut 06880
Equadorian and Greek yarns.
Samples $1.00

Zurcher & Co.
Handwebgarne
CH 3349 Zauggenried
Switzerland
Wools. Sample box $2.00

Dyes

W. Cushing & Co.
North Street
Kennebunkport, Maine 04046
Chemical dyes.

Fezandie & Sperrle
103 Lafayette Street
New York, New York 10013
All types of dyes.

Matheson Dyes and Chemicals
Marion Place
London E81CP, England
All types of dyes.

Wide World of Herbs, Ltd.
11 St. Catherine Street East
Montreal 129, Quebec, Canada
Natural dye materials.

Bibliography

Books

Blackwell, Liz, *A Treasury of Crochet Patterns.* New York; Charles Scribner's Sons, 1971

Davenport, Elsie, *Your Handspinning.* Pacific Grove, California; Craft and Hobby Book Service, 1970

De Dillmont, Therese, *Encyclopedia of Needlework.* Milhouse, France, DMC Library. Also reprinted in paperback by Dover Publications, Inc., 1972.

Feldman, Del Pitt, *Crochet: Discovery and Design.* Garden City, New York; Doubleday & Co., Inc., 1972

Learn How Book. New York; Coats & Clark's Inc.

Lesch, Alma, *Vegetable Dyeing.* New York; Watson-Guptill Publications, 1970

MacKenzie, Clinton D., *New Design in Crochet.* New York; Van Nostrand Reinhold Company, 1972

Mon Tricot, *Knitting Dictionary 1030 Stitches, Patterns, Knitting and Crochet.* New York; Crown Publishers, 1972

Morrow, Susan and Dittrick, Mark, *Contemporary Crochet.* New York; Lancer Books, Inc., 1972

Thomas, Mary, *Mary Thomas's Knitting Book.* New York; Dover Publications, Inc., 1972

Magazines

Craft Horizons, published by The American Crafts Council, 44 West 53rd Street, New York, N.Y. 10019

Handweaver and Craftsman, 220 Fifth Ave., New York, N.Y. 10001

Knitter's Journal, published by *Handweaver and Craftsman*

For British Readers: Books

Kinwood, Jean, *Fashion Crochet.* London; B.T. Batsford Ltd., 1972

Nye, Thelma M., *The Batsford Book of Knitting and Crochet.* London; B.T. Batsford Ltd., 1973

Standing, Dorothy, *New Ways with Crochet.* London; Mills and Boon, 1971

Magazines

Crafts, published by the Crafts Advisory Committee, 28 Haymarket, London SW1Y 4SU

Golden Hands and *Golden Hands Monthly,* published by Marshall Cavendish Ltd., 58 Old Street, London W.1.

Quarterly Journal of the Association of Weavers, Spinners, and Dyers, available from Miss Ruth Hurle, 47 East Street, Saffron Waldon, Essex.

Index

Abstract crochet, 99
Albanian stitch, 26; illus. of, 30

Bags, 94
Bar stitch, 49
Beads, 129
Blanket stitch, 133
Blocking, 86–88
Boots, 95
Buckles, 129
Bump stitch, 49; in sampler, 53

Carding fleece, 13
Chain stitch, 19; illus. of, 23
Circle, 65; illus. of, 69
Clothing, 83; patterns for, 84; yarn for, 86
Cluster stitch, 49; in sampler, 53
Color, 98–99
Cross stitch, 26; illus. of, 31

Decreasing, 65
Design, 99; sources for, 101
Diamond, 65
Double crochet, 26; illus. of, 32–34
Double treble crochet, 27
Dresses, 90

Dye lot, 13
Dyeing yarn, 13

Edging, 54

Figurative crochet, 99
Filet stitch, 47; in sampler, 51
Finger shape, 67; illus. of, 71
Finishing crochet, 41–43
Fleece, 13
Foundation chain, 19; illus. of, 24

Half double crochet, 27; illus. of, 35–36
Hats, 93
Hazelnut stitch, 49; in sampler, 53
Hooks: types of, 11; illus. of, 10

Increasing, 65

Janet stitch, 51; illus. of, 60
Joining pieces of crochet, 49; illus. of, 54–56
Joining yarn, 27, 40–41
Judith stitch, 49; in sampler, 53

Leather, 132–134
Left-handed crocheting, 19

Mittens, 95

Needles, 14

Openwork scallop, 51; illus. of, 57
Oval, 67; illus. of, 70

Pants, 92
Picot stitch, 49; in sampler, 52
Pillow, 67; how to make, 73–77
Ply, definition of, 13
Popcorn stitch, 49; in sampler, 53

Rib stitch, 26; illus. of, 31
Ridge stitch, 26; illus. of, 30
Rotary punch, 132

Sculptural samper, 120–121
Sculpture, 119
Sewing, 49
Sheep, 13
Shell stitch, 47; in samper, 50
Shrimp stitch, 51; illus. of, 59
Single crochet, 26; illus. of, 28–29; to join crochet, 49
Skirts, 88

Sleeves, 91
Slip knot, 19; illus. of, 20
Slip stitch, 27; to join crochet, 49
Snail shape, 67; illus. of, 72
Spindle, 13
Spinning, 13
Spool shape, 65; illus. of, 67
Square, 65; illus. of, 70
Stuffing, 119
Swift, 14

Tapestry stitch, 49; illus. of, 57
Treble crochet, 27; illus. of, 37–39
Triangles, 65; illus. of, 68
Triple treble crochet, 27
Turning chain, 26

Vests, 89

Wool, qualities of, 13

Yarn: chart, 12–13; holding, 19, illus. of,
    21–22; types of, 12; winder, 14
Yarn over, 19

Edited by Jennifer Place
Designed by James Craig and Robert Fillie
Set in 10 point Century Schoolbook by Publishers Graphics, Inc.
Printed by Parish Press, Inc.
Bound by Economy Bookbinding Corp.